'Awaken Your Ancient DNA

Live Fully, Re-Membering Your Wholeness

by Felicity Skye

'Awaken Your Ancient DNA'

by Felicity Skye

Copyright 2013 Felicity Skye

All rights reserved. This book or any portion thereof may not be reproduced or used in any manner whatsoever without the express written permission of the publisher except for the use of brief quotations in a book review or scholarly journal.

First Printing: 2013

ISBN 978-1-291-65056-3

Table of Contents

Introduction

Chapter 1   Earth Star Chakra, page 1

Chapter 2   Base Chakra, page 15

Chapter 3   Sacral Chakra, page 31

Chapter 4   Solar Plexus Chakra, page 50

Chapter 5   Heart Chakra, page 66

Chapter 6   Throat Chakra, page 95

Chapter 7   Third-Eye Chakra, page 117

Chapter 8   Crown Chakra, page 143

Chapter 9   Soul Star Chakra, page 162

Chapter 10   Stellar Gateway Chakra, page 179

Chapter 11   Universal Gateway Chakra, page 197

Chapter 12   Cosmic Gateway Chakra, page 217

Appendix   How to make a Flower Essence, page 240

                    Medicine Wheels, page 242 and 243

                    Chakra chart, page 244

                    About the Author, page 245

                    Bibliography, page 247

Awaken Your Ancient DNA

Live Fully, Re-Membering Your Wholeness

Introduction

Our DNA is our stairway to heaven, a reconnection to our truth, to an ancient wholeness that we have long forgotten. We are so much more than what we perceive ourselves to be and it is time to reawaken the deepest biology of our beingness … our very precious DNA, for it holds the secrets of our soul's light and gifts.

Eons ago, when we were a switched-on race, we had our DNA active and evolving. We worked with the creator and created a spiritually rich existence for ourselves. Everyone worked as one, each had a role they played to create this life and world of spiritually evolved technology, each role as important as the other. Nature was revered as a sacred presence and all life was respected. We worked with angels and other worldly beings to create a heavenly existence. Rituals were common practice as they were understood to activate and safely instigate creative forces of action and manifestation. Sound, colour, angels, crystals and plants were all part of the creator's tool box. As we had a full spectrum of DNA activation, these gifts of the creator carried a more potent energy than they do at this time as we had a more heavenly state of consciousness than we do now. The good news is that it is now time to regain that fuller spectrum again.

Our DNA became lessened when there was a glitch in one of the creations of man in Atlantis. Human ego had started to become separated from the consciousness of the One and man wanted to experiment and play, see what he was capable of. Having 'power' became a sought after commodity and played havoc with the energies of the earth and her magnetic fields. Unbalanced power combined with access to sources of great power usually confined to the evolved and spiritually intelligent human - it was a bad combination. A pyramid designed to perform some sort of new alignment went wrong as it was created for the wrong reasons.

As a result it tore a hole in the bio-magnetic sheath of the planet. This tear created all sorts of major problems like half the earth being covered in water, a loss of memory in man which resulted in a fall from grace. This loss of memory affected our DNA and it had to de-evolve in accordance with the earth's damage. Man had to, more or less, start all over again. Many of the highest Priests and Priestesses of Atlantis knew what was coming and were resituated to the corners of the earth to start new races and carry the seed knowledge of our truth. They have held the earth and us in their care while we began the long journey back to this time of our re-membering. It is time to wake up from the dream, re-educate ourselves and pick up where we left off, remembering all that we have learned so that the same mistakes do not happen again.

The major power points of the earth such as the pyramids, temples and ancient grid lines are all part of the masters plan to hold the earth steady so that we could have the grace to heal and pick up where we left off. They were all ethereally created on the fourth dimension at the time of the destruction and over the years they have been built in our 3D world as conduits of power and energy to feed and stabilise the earth as she healed and re-evolved. They literally are portals of power which is why so many are drawn to them; one feels a certain awakening and shift when around these structures. There is still so much to be learned and as we heal and stabilise our emotions and inner love, compassion and power we will come back into connection with a world we have long been grieving for without even realising that we were grieving.

DNA resides in the nucleus of every cell in our body. It contains our personal blueprint - hair colour, eyes, height and also our genetic inheritance, right down to potential disease patterns. DNA, just like our body, has an aura. The aura registers change first then over a matter of days integrates this change into the physical aspect. Emotions, food, intention, environment and other factors all influence this aura and energetic exchange. As we do our activations we are imprinting this aura energetically, thus beginning a process of deep change.

There are 64 codes that influence this earthly life. There are more but they do not affect your earthly life. They are called DNA light codes. In the etheric our DNA actually hold our complete codes of creation. These are the codes that when activated take us out of duality and back into the One Heart. They allow us to access our past and future knowledge and wisdom, giving us access to the Lightbraries of information in the other realms. This is how we remember who we are and move from separation to unity.

So this is where our DNA healing and reactivation comes in. It is time to get this show back on the road and, for me, all things need to be done with love, fun, ease and grace. Simplicity is always a guide for me. Working with the angels is paramount in this healing, for they are the cosmic paint brush. They are forces of creation, each carrying a different coloured ray, sounds and energy. The angels can reconnect our biology and heal us, they can uplift the vibration of the earth and heal us of our misaligned and unbalanced emotions. Unbalanced emotions can cause all sorts of chaos to erupt; emotion is a powerful force as it is fuelled from the heart with untamed feeling - very potent. We have been going through very powerful experiences for some time now in order to heal our emotional bodies so that we can co- create with the universe, not from our egos, because that's where it all started to go wrong.

Crystals also assist in our realignment with truth; they carry the wisdom of the ages encoded into their matrix, healing systems within systems, connection to Light and specific healing frequencies. I always see crystals as solidified angelic energy.

Essential oils, flower essences and ritual all go towards assisting our healing, of our reconnection and reactivation of the major 12 strands of DNA, which encompass the whole 64. As you start the process you shall find a spiralling effect going on where at times it feels as though you are going over the same old ground again, this is normal as all things have to happen as your nervous system is able to manage, too much light hammering through you too fast and it could overload your system . . . not nice. So be patient, do the work and be kind to yourself. This is a humungous operation you are undertaking - exciting YES - but big. You have probably been going through this emotional healing for some time, preparing yourself for the big shift. Now is the time to bring it all together. Due to planetary alignments, calendar timings and the need for earth changes, the time is now for perfect alignment to support this DNA evolvement. In fact, it is necessary and it is what you came here for now, at this time in history.

With the activation of one's DNA comes the cycling of renewal. This means that one's evolvement will accelerate clearing and cleansing that which no longer resonates with your truth. This is why the goddess rituals and angel invocations are so important, they give you the tools you need to maintain and empower your progress. You probably have begun your ascension process. Most of you would have started some time ago but DNA activation will speed things up. It sort of breaks down old structures that maybe limiting your progress. Always be wise, be gentle, be joyous and loving and attentive to your needs emotional and physical.

Foods that assist with cell/DNA health

We are not only activating our DNA but deeply healing our cellular make up, many of today's power foods and supplements are designed to specifically target this time of deep physical change. Green foods like spirulina and chorella.

Chorella especially has the ability to enter the wall of the cell and renew its integrity. This is so important: every level needs to be addressed in order to integrate a new program into the matrix. This work can affect your make up right down to the death hormone, an old program created by thousands of years of human confusion. It is said we once lived a much longer life than we do now.

Another supplement to look at is alpha lipoic acid.

This is a powerful antioxidant that also can effect in a very positive way the turn over and health of the cell, assisting in a healthy renewal and removal of waste products from the system. It is a powerful antioxidant; it burns up waste products in the body.

Aloe Vera deeply cleanses the tissues of our body, healing and renewing us on every level. She is one of those 'liquid light' products as is chlorophyll. Deep cleansing makes the space for cell renewal to take place.

We don't need to live on these products but it is good measure to think about a maintenance program for yourself.

Probiotics, vitamins and minerals, and the many super foods available on the market today all have a valuable contribution to make towards your ongoing health and transformation. It takes a lot of energy to make deep changes.

A note about angels

There are so many variations on what angel goes where. I have done my best to create a system from material I have read and what my intuition guides me towards. Each angel has their own special place and function; often they can overlap or fulfil the needs of a couple of chakras. This guide will give you a sound basis to work from but if at any time you feel the need of different angels healing attributes in one of your chakras then do invoke them in. There are no hard and fast rules.

Goddess Rituals

The goddess rituals are about bringing new balance to our yin and yang. Males and females are at this time reawakening their inner feminine from her deep slumber. It is important to have creative and joyful ways to keep waking the cells up, to keep healing and raising our vibration. The goddess energy already operates at a high frequency so by working with them they are entraining your energy to a higher frequency.

I have chosen goddesses that I feel offer support to the specific energy of each chakra and DNA level. As much of our healing at this time is concerned with resurrecting the divine feminine aspect within each of us, I have included rituals and ways of working them into our daily lives. Ritual and action set in motion an integration of these archetypal energies, to influence the awakening of your Light Codes. We need to have ways of integrating these new ways of being, of retraining ourselves to operate as a divine being, honouring life and the earth. When we do this, when we become this goddess ourselves we have imprinted and reawakened what already lies within us but we do need to retrain the way we operate. These goddess deities will help us see how to do this, that is why they exist, to help human kind evolve and return to a race of divine beings.

We are creating new neural pathways in our brains, turning the tracks in a new direction. The old pathways are habitual ways of thinking and behaving, how we react to certain situations, digest food and ideas, everything about how you integrate life. You can imagine how much focus and intent it takes to imprint new ways of being, to imprint new neural pathways of evolved integration of life.

The chakras/layers of DNA and activation occur in groups. Within each major layer of the 12 is found a certain number of light codes.

Earthstar chakra: DNA core

Base Chakra: 1 and 2

Sacral chakra: 3 and 4

Solar chakra: 5

Heart and Higher heart chakras: 6 and 7

Throat chakra: 8 and 9

Third Eye chakra: 10

Crown chakra: 11 and 12

Soul Star chakra: 13 to 24

Stellar Gateway chakra: 25 to 36

Universal Gateway chakra: 37 to 48

Cosmic Gateway chakra: 49 to 64

The Light Codes carry so much of our ancient memories. As we activate consciously each of the DNA layers we also activate the light codes, turning up the dimmer switch, allowing more light to enter our beingness. This all happens as we are able to hold and manage new levels of light. Our nervous system needs to be strong, as does our grounding and physical health. Knowledge heals, it allows the pathways to safely heal and clear. This is why we address our healing and rebuilding in several ways, to ensure a safe and healthy passage through this mighty and exciting opening.

"In the seamless space of existence you cannot intellectualise evolution.

Do the works then surrender into your liquid silence and God self.

Trust and become one with the divine intelligence that knows your truth, your sound and potentiality

Allow and float in a clear sea of unknowingness, feel the fear, then release even more deeply into this seamless bliss, for my embrace is ever present."

As we work with the energies of each chakra, using the tools provided, we send a ripple effect through our chakras, our DNA and light codes, awakening them from their slumber and reactivating their full potential. Be patient with yourself and above all enjoy yourself. Love and joy are the key components . . . so indulge.

The Sigils and the Order of the Rose

The sigils that come with each angel and goddess are an energetic signature of their essence. The masters and many of the goddesses are a part of "The Order of the Rose". "The Order of the Rose" is a group of evolved masters who are specifically working with us to raise our vibration and ascend ourselves and the earth. They came to me when I first started making the essences and have been guiding me in this work ever since. Through the essences, rituals and sigils they have created a system where we can access their energy into our lives more easily, assisting us to heal and accelerate our progress. The sigils are based on an ancient magical alphabet, blended with my perception and artistic grace. These sigils can be used in many magical and healing ways. They provide access to the angels, goddesses and masters' sacred energy, bypassing the mind and opening up their field of light to enhance your work.

They can be used like a reiki symbol in healing to place the energy of the angel into a specific chakra, bringing the angels special gifts of healing.

Inscribe them on candles for invoking their magical attributes to your workings.

Drawn on paper and placed under your glass of water to imbue the water with healing energy.

A more specific description and use will be offered with each chapter.

Chapter 1

Earth - Star Chakra

Archangel Sandalphon

Your Earth Star chakra is your connection to the earth grid. It anchors your soul into your body allowing your essence to have a physical experience. If the Earth Star is not tended to lovingly you will become a lost soul, unable to follow and fulfil your creative goals. The Earth Star seems to ground and then magnetise all you need to create and manifest your desires. It provides a capability and vital energy to feed your goals that are directed and fed to you from your soul. As we raise our vibration we also raise the vibration of the planet as we are one. It is a bit like having good healthy soil so that your roots can anchor and grow a healthy and abundant life.

The sacred geometry of this chakra is a cube, very stable and supportive.

This chakra also creates a triangular point at the bottom of the merkabah and so unifies the upper transpersonal chakras with the lower personal chakras. As this connection strengthens Source energy is able to pour through us to restore harmony on planet earth. The earth spirits such as the elementals and devas of the planet then also start to come back into a more substantial role, turning our planet once more into a Garden of Eden. A true sense of the One Heart coming back into manifested reality; it is also a realignment of the duality of male/female energies which creates a whole new balance of earth's energy and universal alignment. Shifts of this magnitude can cause quakes and earth changes as she also struggles to realign her biomagnetic fields. As our biomagnetic field rebalances to an alignment with our true self, we start to regain our soul memories; we just know stuff and find it easier to act on our knowing. This is our re-membering; this is what it is all about.

It is so important to LOVE life, to do things you love. It's like permission to spoil ourselves, have fun, laugh and dream. All these things feed you into your Earth Star, strengthening your joy factor that then increases your life force and anchoring of it into this chakra. Everyone, without any exceptions has a life mission to fulfil; there will be lessons to be learned and challenges to over come. Some, hopefully most, can deal with this but unfortunately some can't due to their ego or maybe lack of will to live, maybe too weak to handle the challenge side of things, they seek escapism, become ungrounded. Before you know it they are off their path, dancing in fields of illusion and untruth. These fields of illusion are an astral creation of their minds, it seems so real but it is a reality they are creating to support their belief system. Once they are enmeshed in this space it is hard to come out, sometimes a traumatic experience will smash the dream and the ensuing healing can get them back on track.

The Earth Star will continue to ground more and more of your evolving self as you heal and reactivate your highest potential. Massage, chakra balancing and healings are all great supportive measures to keep the channels and meridians of your body flowing so that the energy continues to ground. The lower chakras can be a little slower at processing so just keep an eye on how you are feeling.

This chakra is a rather vulnerable one. The angels have shown me that bullying, self doubt, or unpleasant intent from another can all weaken this chakra. If someone wanted to undermine another, this is a great way to do it, as the poor victim will wander around lost and unable to express their brilliance. Magicians of old knew this and used it as a way to stop their peers from outdoing them, undermining their power. No grounding - no power! No manifestation of greatness. So now and then check in, clear any old programs that may linger here. They can travel with you through the hologram of existence, maybe a curse from centuries ago but there is no need to fulfil it anymore.

Signs of unbalance here are sluggishness, heaviness, fatigue, lack of motivation, couch potato, light headed, not with it, nervy, anxious, cannot manifest.

A healthy Earth Star leaves you feeling vital, positive, and healthy, grounded, connected to earth divas, in tune with self and universal self, manifesting well.

Archangel Sandalphon

Archangel Sandalphon is the angel who works with the Earth Star chakra. He is the twin of Archangel Metatron who holds the Stellar Gateway open, they work together to assist in the anchoring of your divine blueprint into form. He feels like such a warm loving presence, strong and yet gentle, lovingly coaxing us into our earthly lives, making the transition as comfy as possible. I always think of him when I smell sandalwood oil, apart from the name similarities. Sandalwood is so warm and smooth, very soothing and woody, spiritually grounding and protective just like Sandalphon.

Sandalphon and Metatron work together to bring cohesion to the Soul Star chakra and Earth Star chakras. Sandalphon governs the transformation of the electrical energies that generate from the Earth, making connection with the cosmic matrix. Metatron facilitates the magnetic energies drawn from the galaxy to Planet Earth, which create alignment with the Planetary Matrix. These dual forces flow through the form and symbol of the infinity, circling within a figure eight, like a constant two-way flow of energy and information, looping as it were in rhythmic harmony between Heaven and Earth. This action takes place within you and also at power points upon the Earth where the heavenly and earthly forces powerfully anchor in together to broadcast specific vital information into our planetary intelligence. That is why ritual is often done in such places as the pyramids, Stonehenge and other sacred sites.

Crystals

This is a selection of crystals that will work well to activate, balance and bring healing to your Earth Star chakra.

Black Tourmaline is one of my favourite crystals. It is black with striations running down the side of it, the striations carry the energy straight down through your chakra, connecting to you nervous system and draws out all negativity from the chakra.

This is also a very protective stone, it creates a force field that deflects negativity and provides a safe and grounded environment for you to move around.

Assists in the clearing of scattered thinking and actions, bringing you back to reality.

It also assists to deflect electromagnetic pollution which can significantly zap your energy leaving you weakened and vulnerable.

Hematite is very grounding and calming. This stone can find you and bring your focus back to the here and now - very handy.

Its lovely mirrored surface deflects interference, can be used as a scrying tool and brings light into the deeper regions.

The centre of hematite is red, so it is a wonderful blood tonic; it draws out disease and assists with muscle weakness.

Another interesting attribute is that it grounds and protects the body if you do deep meditation or astral travelling. This allows one to let go more easily in deep trance work.

Smokey Quartz literally draws the heaviness out of one and carries it into the earth for healing.

She carries the light of quartz and the smoky darkness, a powerful combination. This allows the light to be carried very deeply into the core of self. As she travels deeply within she is then able to dislodge toxins from the deeper subterranean spaces of your body, so important when dealing with the lower chakras as they burn deeper into the body with their imprinting. Smokey will scour out those hidden toxins so more light can penetrate into your Earth Star, offering protection as it does so. More light means more soul energy grounding into the physical.

Rainbow Obsidian, as the name implies, carries the spectrum of colour within it, drawing all the healing rays into your Earth Star to deeply balance and align with the earth and the angels.

Its volcanic origins give it great power and gusto to empower your chakra with plenty of energy and power.

This in turn gets it working at full potential for your creative implementation.

Petrified Wood, a tree turned to stone, is quite amazing. The combination creates a wonderfully grounding stone. It is ancient and solid, the roots of which travel deep into the earth so it makes a great stone to bring the comfort and strength of a tree with the solidness of a stone. Assists to strengthen the bones affected by a weak Earth Star chakra. This ancient being brings vitality drawn from deep within the earth, assisting with chronic fatigue issues.

Tibetan Quartz contains both clear quartz and black inclusions and is usually double terminated so it would hold both the Soul Star and Earth Star in balance. By placing this stone on the body I feel it would activate and bring the two of them into synchronisation with each other, create that magnetic pole. Two in one, by having the light and dark in the same stone the harmony would be awesome, great for carrying with you into challenging spaces.

Other crystals that were shown to me for this chakra were moldavite and peach selenite. They seem to be specifically for star seeds.

Moldavite is a form of obsidian also, originating from comet particles. It carries a very high vibration and would initially appear to be for the higher chakras but what it does is bring one's starry origins into the physical body deeply. Many star seeds find earthly life quite challenging, their upper chakras much bigger than their earth chakras, which leaves them a little ungrounded and appearing like space cadets or sometimes Indigo people. Moldavite allows them to feel grounded and at home in their bodies, reconnected to their higher chakras but in a much more grounded way. This then allows their amazing creative minds and visions to safely channel into their lives. The green colour makes it a tonic for the heart also, opening the heart to embrace oneself.

Peach Selenite. This form of selenite also carries a high vibration. Selenite has the ability to align your physical structure-spine, bones, nervous system and muscles - as well as your spiritual body, connecting you physically and spiritually. The peach colour assists the energy to penetrate the Earth Star. It strengthens the heart connection to life making it a joy to be here.

Apart from the selenite any of these stones can be used as an essence, although moldavite is very powerful used this way and I tend to only use it this way as a meditation, vision tonic. Selenite makes a wonderful meditation stone, either laid on the body or held with intention.

The crystals can also be laid on the body in a crystal layout healing, either below the feet or between them.

Flower Essence for Earth Star

Ironbark Gum Tree

An ancient guardian of the earth, Ironbark stands so powerfully, offering us support and an awakening of our inner power. Working with this ancient being was very humbling.

Works to strengthen one's connection to the earth plane, anchoring in the Soul Star.

Offers support for ideas, providing strong foundations for their manifestation.

She provides a strong field of light, revealing where the best way forward lies and revealing any negative attachments, cleansing and purifying your spiritual root system of any interference.

The essence connects with the ancient elders of the land, tapping into an age old source of protection and support. These elders understand the magics of the land and how they have been misused, so they are able to clear and vitalise your essence with pure earth energy.

Strengthens the liver meridian, kidneys and adrenals.

Essential Oils for the Earth Star

Vetiver has a very earthy musky smell as she is made from the roots of a grass. Vetiver is very grounding and supportive; she tends to self-correct your energy when it is being compromised by a situation, holding you solidly together. Helps to reduce stress and fear and assists in manifesting your physical needs. Place a drop on the bottom of your foot to stabilise your energy.

Myrrh is slightly musty and earthy; it is a resin from a tree, so once again travels deep. She heals our deep wounds; these wounds can often be unknown to us which tends to make them even more under-mining to our forward movement. Myrrh works deeply to assist in the unfolding of and healing of these wounds, leading to forgiveness and completion. Works like a disinfectant, going to were she is needed.

This lovely essence can be used topically or as incense in ritual.

Sandalwood. Many would say this is a higher chakra oil but it is also made from the wood of a tree. It is such sacred oil, so calming and uplifting, I feel it brings the sacred into our earthly existence which is what this chakra is all about. Sandalwood is quite an all rounder, universal oil/incense. Sandalwood provides a calming effect, easing fears and bringing a certain joy to being alive.

A prayer of protection to say before any ritual or healing:

"In the name of love and light, I ask Archangel Michael to surround me and fill me with your divine light of protection; I ask that the heavenly light of angels surround the space in which I work, creating a space of highest light allowing us/me to work safely and for the highest good of all. Please move all negative energy back into the light for healing. God Bless and thank you."

Ritual of Activation and Earth Star Healing

A black or red candle

Some myrrh or sandalwood incense to uplift the space

Essential oil to place on feet or on candle

Earth Star symbol

Your chosen crystal

Inscribe angel sigil on candle and dress with chosen oil then place in a safe dish

Say prayer of protection

Place crystal at your feet or near candle

Smudge yourself with sage, sandalwood or myrrh incense

Take a couple of drops of the essence, either a crystal or flower essence. This can also be placed below your feet to directly access the chakra point. Don't worry if you don't have an essence as the process will still work. An essence does provide ongoing support.

Put yourself into a relaxed state, doing some nice even breaths and calm your mind, bringing yourself into the present moment.

Invoke Archangel Sandalphon by saying:

"I now lovingly ask my guides, celestial helpers and Archangel Sandalphon to activate, open and strengthen my Earth Star chakra, placing within it the crystalline structures and sacred geometry I need to fully bring my Earth Star chakra into its highest vibration and healthy activation. I ask this so that I may now ground my Stellar Gateway and Soul Star into my physical life in a healthy and balanced way, drawing my souls light into my life's expression allowing me to fulfil my divine mission. I ask for this to happen on every level of my light body, through every cell and DNA code now.

Thank you and blessings

May I live in peace.

Om Mani Padmi Hum."

Feel your Earth Star beneath your feet, gently pulsing with energy and love, feel your body coming into rhythm with it, allow yourself all the time you need as your soul comes into contact through your physical body and anchors into your Earth Star chakra. Your guides are ensuring a safe passage and rebirthing.

Sit with this for as long as you like, feeling the beautiful energy of Sandalphon and your guides working to bring this healing in for you.

Write any messages or insights you receive down in a journal, as it helps to refer back to this as you go through the healing that follows. Be aware, as these rituals don't just affect your physical body but may manifest as incidents in your life to bring awareness to situations and old programs that need addressing. Also one's dreams may have messages.

Animal totem

Rainbow Serpent

He travels deep within the earth, shifting and energising the lay lines and grounding the spirits of the land. Earth devas and elementals are activated by the serpent's realigning of the sacred pathways of evolution. As our chakra systems become more aligned with divine truth then he accordingly opens these sacred, ancient doorways, allowing more and more magic to re-enter our lives.

The sound of didgeridoo music is very grounding; earthy sounds tune your Earth Star up.

Uluru is such a powerful portal, all that rock and ancient spiritual history. As you come into contact with it, the energy is so grounding that you automatically open up to download all that you are able to embody in the way of spiritual energy. You get to feel the immense field of light that you are. She is an immense library of ancient history and knowledge; we are so blessed to have such an amazing landmark in Australia. Uluru's role here is yet to be fully understood but I feel she is holding the space for the knowledge of an ancient civilisation to be reborn here, within us. She is an ancient guardian spirit of the earth, holding immense energy stable for us as we become capable of becoming our ancient memories again. I am being told she has ancient connections to Tibet and to the Pleiadian star system, a portal of communication and entry.

Goddess Work

Persephone

A Goddess to work with here is Persephone, as she descends into the depths of the earth then returns, transformed and fertile. She shows us how to die to the old and return over and over again, renewed and reborn, safely held in the arms of love.

Pomegranates are Persephone's food. They symbolise fertility, are a deep red and bursting full of seeds.

Enjoy one, sucking the sweet juice and then throwing the seeds to the wind and visualising your dreams taking root and growing into reality, big and strong like a tree. Allow the energy of the pomegranate to clear and protect your visions.

Ask Persephone to assist you to keep moving through the ebb and flow of your growth and to show you the way back home to your heart.

Drink the juice with intention; allow her rich antioxidants to dissolve any blocks you have, returning vibrancy to all that you do.

Write any challenges down on a piece of paper and either burn it or bury it somewhere special; knowing you have now released it to the underworld for healing and resolution.

Plant seeds with intention, feeling the earth, smelling the earth. You will feel an easing of your energy as she graciously relieves you of excess static that can be causing ungroundedness in your energy. You will also be growing new roots as you watch your plants prosper.

Visualise your Earth Star as a pomegranate, round, shiny, full, dark, fertile with seeds; see her glowing below your feet. Now see her seeds all bursting forth, shooting off in all directions, travelling deep within the earth, carrying all your dreams and longings. Feel the earth reaching out and nurturing these seeds, nourishing your dreams, protected in her deep, dark womb and finally sprouting forth upon the earth. All of them strong and healthy, born at the exact right time in the exact right space. Trust mother earth to protect and know exactly how to assist your fullness of being and to fulfil your creative self.

Durga

Durga is an Indian goddess of powerful feminine protection - for men and women. Chanting her mantra builds a profound, vibrational protective armour that shrugs off any attempt at undermining our power, either from ourselves or another. This profound mantra creates a field of proactive intelligence that sorts the negative thoughts and floating energy out for us.

"Om Dum Durgayei Namaha"

(Om Doom Door-gah-yea Nahm-ah hah)

"Salutations to She who is beautiful, to the seeker of truth and terrible to those who would injure devotees of truth".

Light a black candle, carve Durga's name in the wax. As you chant her mantra, see the black of the wax and the light of the flame holding your Earth Star and Soul Star chakras in alignment, feel your stillness and strength flowing through you. All problems and confusions dissolving in the light as your auric field expands, clears and glows with truth, love and powerful protective light.

Working with Durga and chanting her mantra will break up dark crystallised energy, dispersing it back into the Light. This is a very powerful mantra to be used with respect. It not only breaks up internal blocks but will assist in clearing situations that no longer serve your highest good. Offer her marigolds or mangoes and good incense when doing a formal healing chant. In doing this you honour her presence and feed the energy.

Summary of Earth Star Chakra

The Earth Star chakra does not work with any Light Codes specifically but creates the core structure of each one. It appears to be the grounding force of the soul, right down to the infinitesimal core of the DNA structure and health. This chakra holds the show together, nourishing and creating a solid base for activation of the whole spectrum of Light Codes . . . a big job.

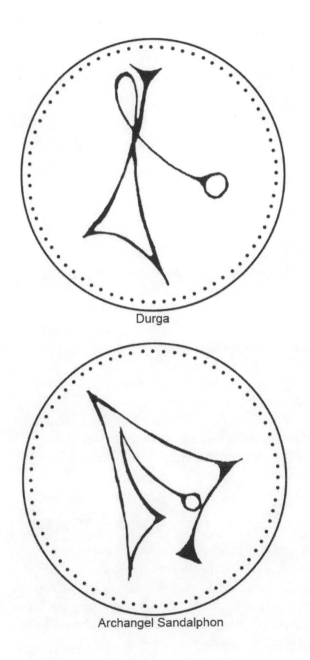

Chapter 2

Base Chakra

1st and 2nd Light Codes

Associated parts of the body are the testes, ovaries, spinal column, bones, immune system, legs and feet, anus.

The Base Chakra is found at the base of the spine around the coccyx. When doing a healing you can access it over the pubis or by placing a crystal between the legs. Where the Earth Star is the root of the soul, the Base Chakra is the root of the physical body in the third dimension. It focuses on our physical life and deals with survival, endurance, and grounding, maintaining and nourishing our vital force. It is associated with our adrenals and sexual glands. The first ten years of your life build the foundation from which you act and react for the rest of your life.

How we focus on and achieve our goals is developed here. The Base Chakra connects us to the planet's resources and also to the tribe or clan. Having a strong connection to the tribe gives one a sense of belonging; it empowers one to believe in oneself and to draw from that energy to manifest. A strong Base Chakra will create a vital human being with strong life force and many resources to draw from. All the support they need to be successful will just appear as if by magic to create their potential.

Low life force and no sense of belonging obviously create the opposite. Struggle, health issues, depression and most often deep-seated fears, probably programmed in during those first vital ten years. Fear of death is a major issue here as this separates one from life, for death is a part of life. There will probably be past life issues of traumatic death here. Sexual interference as a child, I believe, also interferes dramatically with the health of this chakra. Disconnection from self can occur due to the myriad number of emotions that such an experience can cause.

So while I believe it is important to work with these injuries in order to heal them, we must not linger on them but keep upgrading our system and putting good healthy healing energy into them. Remember: it is light infused experiences that feed and open our receptors. Finding creative ways to heal and delete the old programs and wounds is a positive and creative way to heal. Endless lingering over the unfairness of life is not going to get you anywhere.

The Base Chakra is actually the physical seat of the awakening kundalini. It is from here that the energy builds, when one feels a sense of totality within oneself. It starts a fire that needs no "other" to stoke, and it begins its climb up the spine. This chakra is a very physical chakra but seems to hold the key to our powerful spiritual experiences.

Sexual issues can come up here, like how strong the sexual urge is and how much energy can feed it. Sexuality is life force, like any force it can be used positively or negatively, when experienced with a beloved other it can cause an immense spiritual experience of oneness and love, every cell in the body vibrating with sublime love energy, releasing wonderfully healing hormones, nourishing the whole body. When the base energy is low sexual interest may also lag which can be experienced as a low ability to manifest.

We also find sexual issues in the sacral chakra but more of an emotional nature, so they can bleed into each other, maybe covering a different aspect of the same issue. The adrenals are I believe effected by base issues but they also come up in solar plexus health, so keep an open mind as there seems to be a lot of flexibility in our make up. Use your own intuition as to how to work with different issues to bring back harmony. This is why different angels, oils and crystals may be used at different times for different issues.

A balanced Base Chakra has solid foundations, physical and emotional needs met, food, clothing, housing, good sustainability. Manifests easily, healthy life force, good blood and healthy bones, healthy sex drive and balanced emotional make up

Unbalanced Base Chakra is ungrounded, low energy, always wanting more, either no sex drive or a sexual addict, could be someone who is draining to be around, sluggish bowel as they are unable to process either food or emotional toxins, lacking in trust.

This chakra is a beautiful glowing red lotus when it is healthy and vibrant with life force, fuelling the other chakras with good positive and nourishing energy.

It is here that we begin to delete our fear of death, minimising it so that eventually the death hormone becomes weaker and we can maintain our youthfulness for longer and eventually overcome the death hormone and realise ourselves as immortal. That may take a couple of generations - or not.

Light Codes 1-2

The 1st and 2nd light codes are about not living in fear around our survival anymore, issues to do with money, relationships and basically all Base Chakra issues. As these heal so too will our body start to feel more alive, healing our fear impulse will release a deep inner flow of energy that has the potential to speed up our ascension process dramatically. Our systems would be able to synchronise with our higher knowing and inner healer enabling us to live at our full potential. If all Light Codes live in every cell then as we disable another major program our whole system and potential accelerates towards a better life experience. The dimmer switch can go up and down, especially when we are clearing and processing another layer of old stuff. Eventually they stay turned on and we are in a constant state of co-creation with our Source.

Archangels Anael and Azrael

I feel both these angels have a place here. As I describe each of their gifts you will be able to discern which one is most appropriate to invoke for the healing at hand.

For a general healing in your practice or upon yourself, Anael is the usual one.

Archangel Anael

Anael is called the fire filled sacred warrior. His red ruby ray intensifies the energy of the Base Chakra, imbuing it with health and vitality. He brings warrior energy, not one of anger but of strength that can deal with life's challenges, assisting us to find the energy and will to keep going. Courage to overcome issues that arise and to move past fears that may intimidate us and hold us back from fulfilment. He assists our spiritual muscles to be in peak condition.

Anael can foster a sense of direction, friendships, integrity and hope. His name means 'glory of the divine', thus inspiring us to fulfil our soul's mission, giving us the Source energy to meet the challenges and over come any fears. Fears can be lodged in our cellular make up; they may unconsciously be causing things to slow down that once looked so exciting. They may be the result of doing things that in other times have led us into painful situations such as death or we made vows to hold ourselves back, all these can have some invisible effect on our energy, causing us to feel uncomfortable about following our higher destiny. Anael can help us to find the courage to face our inner devil and keep on going.

Anael will also infuse your beingness with pure, vital energy. This can assist in the healing of illness and also give a great boost to one's sexual drive. Libido can be a sensitive thing, especially when there is so much change going on. Our Base Chakra is working so hard at this time to continually process so much stuff for us and keep on grounding in our new level of self. The Earth Star is also part of this grounding process, continually grounding the old and drawing in more and more of your enlightened spirit. So a good boost of Anael's pure ruby energy is a welcome treat, giving energy to help on all levels of your personal journey and at the same time planting some lovely rich rays into the earth. The rich energy of Anael gives a wonderful boost to one's lower endocrine glands such as ovaries/testes and adrenal glands which in turn feeds the whole system which stimulates youthfulness and vitality. He keeps our hearts connected to life, a valuable addition when one's has closed down and shielded up due to an overload of sensory pain.

Another important attribute of the angel's presence is his ability to dissolve the sense of separateness. The Base Chakra is all about the tribe and belonging so this can help when one suffers from aloneness, for we all need each other to drive this ship home. Freedom and liberation are our birth right and it is now time to dissolve all sadness, fear and despair and reclaim our true sovereignty. Anael is a great angel to call on generally to just make this transition so much easier, offering vitality, strength, an open heart and the endurance to keep going.

Archangel Azrael

This angel is known as the 'angel of death'. He accompanies the departing soul as its body dies, assisting them to pass over, offering comfort and protection.

Azrael will assist with all transitions, such as a new job, new child, new home, anything that requires a letting go and moving on. It is in the Base Chakra that we hang on out of anxiety and fear of the unknown. He also assists people who are caring for seriously ill people, easing the pain of their passing. He also makes a great assistant to grief councillors.

With so much change being required of us this life time I think he makes a great ally to call on. He can assist with any old fears around death that may be weakening your lower chakras and so affecting your life force.

If you work with Australian Bush Flower Essences: Bottlebrush and Bush Iris would be his essences.

Base Chakra Crystals

Ruby is so rich and red and carries a vibrant royal energy, clearing all fears and unbalanced energies leaving a lively sparkling energy in her place. She infuses a passion for life, her royal energy guiding you towards your highest expression and clearing away that which would stand in your way. Ruby will build your sexual energy after a time of lowered interest. Motivation and enthusiasm are her trademarks - whatever you are contemplating!

Garnet is another highly energising stone. She builds stamina and passion, lending a drive to get things done. Inspiration and ideas come in and the energy to fulfil them. She removes blocks assisting one to be grounded and vital all at once. This high energy vitalises the reproductive organs increasing fertility and sexual interest. Garnet helps one to manifest one's hopes and dreams.

Agate has many varieties and they all have a healing effect on the Base Chakra. This can range from calming to grounding. She is such a beautiful earth stone; she brings a lovely range of minerals with her different shades and varieties. Agate is a good general chakra balancer.

Red Jasper is also a calming, nourishing stone. She builds energy but in a gentle nurturing way and we all need nurturing here sometimes. Red jasper will offer motivation to follow through on creative projects in a calm way and a protective warm energy to surround you in times of need.

Red Calcite helps with panic attacks and ADHD, reducing anxiety and replacing it with a calm, easy energy. Also good for the kidneys.

Smokey Quartz will assist a breaking down of these toxins and help to clear them off back to ground level. I am adding her here as well as often the Base Chakra needs help to detox old programs and toxic build up. So check in and see just what is needed in the moment.

The Base Chakra holds a lot of our soul and genetic memories, some need healing and clearing, others need awakening. Awakening often needs the power of the red stones, to heal and stimulate but old traumas may need one of the darker stones to break it up and assist in its removal.

So any of the Earth Star crystals can be used here also as their functions are not so dissimilar, each grounding an aspect of you.

All these stones can be used in crystal waters for added healing effect.

Make room sprays, great for your work area to uplift and add stimulating energy.

Flower Essence-Base Chakra

Red Hibiscus

Just looking at a red Hibiscus is a lush and sensual experience. She is so open and vibrant, her pollen rich stamen reaching out inviting all to sip of her nectar and be brushed by her golden light. The petals look so open and trusting, open to all the delights life has to offer. When I see Hibiscus I always feel a connection to Pele, a goddess of Hawaii and volcanoes, so much passion and powerful earth energy but coupled with exotic goddess beauty.

Heals separation and insecurity issues.

Imbues one with life-force and vitality.

Very Goddessy, giving sexual self confidence.

Energizes pelvic organs.

Motivating, assisting one to take action on dreams.

Builds charisma and magnetic energy to manifest one's dreams.

Great essence for dancers, bringing in abundant and vital energy.

Use in love and abundance magic.

Opens Base Chakra like a flower, drawing love into oneself from the earth, thus creating a pathway forward based on self love and loving experiences.

This loving opening then heals issues of fear and lack of confidence.

Essential Oils for Base Chakra

Patchouli has an earthy scent which is great for grounding. It has a balancing effect, assisting stress related disorders. She is also an aphrodisiac, stimulating those vital lower organs. A small amount goes a long way, too much can be very stimulating. It is a natural antibiotic, beneficial for fungal infections and athlete's foot. Think about it: Candida is fungal and usually grows in low energy people, so this oil could provide healing on a couple of levels. Added to carrier oil, a small amount on the bottom of your foot can be very beneficial, grounding, healing and attracting good energy, as she is known magically for attracting wealth and passion.

Cedar wood is so strengthening, centreing and grounding. I love cedar wood. Such a majestic tree automatically has you standing stronger and confidently. She brings the angels of purification close to you, thus clearing physical and emotional issues. Cedar is antiseptic and very protective. I used her on the feet of someone who had a bad experience with drugs that left her very ungrounded and lost. Within minutes she was back and feeling more in her body again and able to cope. Cedar clears the way; no one messes with her strong presence. Can be used on the feet and also a little on the solar plexus as this goes a long way towards instilling confidence and a shield of light. I see such trees as master earth beings and their assistance is very special.

Spikenard is the oil Mary anointed Jesus feet with before he was beaten by Roman soldiers. It contains valeranone, one of the ingredients in valerian. This is a sleep aid and muscle relaxant, so makes a great calming aid giving those adrenals a rest from continual fight and flight. The fight and flight reflex can get locked on after a time of stress thus draining the energy out of your adrenal battery. These oils can provide great relief by rebooting your life force and vital energy.

Ritual of Activation and healing for Base Chakra

A red candle

Sage or Myrrh to cleanse

Essential oil to dress candle and place on body

AA Anael's sigil

Chosen crystal

Place candle dressed in oil on a safe container and light it

Say prayer of protection

Have card with angel sigil in front of this, under candle or placed on your Base Chakra if laying down doing a healing. Engrave the sigil on the candle for added benefit.

Place crystal on card or chakra

Smudge space to purify. Another option is burning some oil in an oil burner or finding a pure and appropriate incense

Take a couple of drops of the flower essence or place a drop on Base Chakra
Put yourself into a relaxed state, do some deep easy breaths,

calming and clearing your mind of all but what you are doing now.

To invoke Archangel Anael

"In the name of love I ask my guides, celestial helpers and Archangel Anael to please open, activate and balance my Base Chakra, placing within it the crystalline structures and sacred geometry I need to fully bring my Base Chakra into its highest vibration and health activation. I ask that the corresponding Light Codes 1 through to 2 and DNA be brought into perfect harmony with my soul's highest expression now. I command the activation of the 1st and 2nd light codes now, bringing them to their highest level of presence on every level of my light body and through every chakra and bodily system now. I ask that all of my light codes come into harmony with each other, each supporting the harmonious action of the other as a unified whole. I am so grateful for this healing. Thank you, Om Mani Padmi Hum."

Sit or lie quietly and allow the energy to do its work.

Breathe into your Base Chakra, feel the energy growing stronger and pulsing with a vibrant red glow. Take your time; sink deeper and deeper into this healing space, give the angels and guides time to do their work. This could be a lovely exercise before sleep so that the process can work through the night.

Write down any insights you may receive.

Extinguish the candle and give thanks for the healing. This effectively closes the energy down.

Prayer to invoke Archangel Azrael

"In the name of love I invoke Archangel Azrael to assist me with the transition I am going through at this time, please help me to flow with these shifts, clearing and healing any resistance I may be holding onto to do with these changes. Please assist all

concerned here to feel at peace and full of grace.

Blessings, Om Mani Padmi Hum."

The seed sound for the Base Chakra is *Lam* (Lahm)

Chanting this sound silently or vocally will assist with bringing this chakra into balance.

Animal Totem

An animal totem for this chakra would be the turtle. They are age-old and so beautiful. They move on land as well as in water, carrying their home everywhere they go. We must learn that we are always home and not long for some mythical home we feel lies separate from us as this leads to ungroundedness and dissipation of energy. I have heard of a tribe of Aboriginals called the Turtle Tribe who live from the land, peacefully being in the moment, feeding from the land and leaving very little footprint of destruction in their wake. Even in our urban style of living we can learn to live harmoniously with the earth, giving and honouring all life.

The elephant is another Base Chakra animal and working with Ganesh the elephant headed God is worthwhile to clear obstacles and create opportunity.

Drumming is great Base Chakra music for healing and energising, really puts us back in our body. The sound connects to Mother Earth's heart beat, putting us back into rhythm with life and nourishment. Her heart beat can reset our body's rhythm assisting all our physical systems to work harmoniously with the rhythms of the earth. As we reconnect with the earth this way we raise our frequency allowing an opening of the higher dimensions, activating the elemental kingdoms and their divine rays of creation. The spectrum of colours will grow brighter and magic will resurface.

Ganesh

Ganesh is a powerful god to work with; he assists us to shift the heavier road blocks we can come across as we ascend our personal spirals. He is known as the elephant headed god and is very revered in India. Ganesh symbolises cosmic unity and consciousness, his mission is to work with us in clearing the heavier underside so that we can once again reach for the stars. The lower Light Codes and chakras tend to hold the heavier programs.

His mantra is used to clear obstacles:

"Om Gum Ganapatayei Namaha."

(Om Gum Guh-Nuh-Puh-Tuh-Yei Nahm-Ah-Ha)

(Om and salutations to the remover of obstacles for which Gum is the seed.)

Goddess Work

Gaia is the name given to the Earth Goddess. As the Base Chakra is directly connected to our physical body and the Earth is our physical home it seems proper that we honour Gaia as our goddess here.

Picture a voluptuous, bosomy woman, holding us all in the depth of her deep heart's song, cradling us as we grow into our spiritual adult hood. She has loved us and stayed faithful to us through so much war, rape and pillage, as we fought our way back to our re-membering. Gaia is the epitome of unconditional love.

If we are not grounded in a healthy way, our higher chakras cannot ground into our physical experience, grounding really is the key to evolving in a strong and healthy way.

Place offerings of flowers on an altar out in your garden or in a park somewhere.

Begin by saying:

"Beautiful Gaia

Mother's song

Open my heart

Help me belong."

Lay yourself on the earth, breathe rhythmically, tuning into her heart beat, connect and allow yourself to feel supported, understood, loved and accepted just as you are. Feel any stress or sadness you have carried being dissolved by her loving touch, allowing yourself to be cradled and supported.

Sit on the earth and feel your tail bone extending into the earth, grounding any excess old energy away. The rich minerals of the earth will transmute the old energy into fresh new available energy. Feel your cord extending right down to the core of the earth then allow the energy of her heart and power to rise up your cord and energise your body, feel it rising right up through your spine, your chakras and out into the space surrounding you, creating a wonderful bubble of healing and protection. Visualise it forming a balloon of light around your body, strong, buoyant and bright, protecting your energy and keeping you clear and strong.

Stand and once again run your energy down into the heart of the earth, feel the warm, rich earth, full of minerals, crystals, tree roots and underground streams. Keep it running until you feel it pause, be still then feel it start to draw energy back up your cord, pulsing with life-force, bringing all those nourishing minerals with it, feeding your chakras and body. Feel it rise out above your head, connecting with your upper chakras and then descending back into the earth, taking the wonderful Light back with it, planting this Light deep within the Earth for you, uniting heaven and earth.

Some spots work better for this than others as they have access to natural healing veins or vortexes of energy, feel around and experience the difference that a different location can make.

These exercises not only strengthen our physical, emotional and spiritual bodies but they also raise the vibration of the Earth and assist in the dimensional doorways opening in a healthy and safe way. The more aligned with Light and inner power we become so too does the Earth for we are her conduits of Light and hold the ship steady while she ascends. If we wobble so too does she. This is quite a responsibility.

Sometimes fatigue can be experienced after these awakenings as the body needs time to assimilate new frequencies coming in, realigning all your bodies into a higher state of awareness. With the first chakra the adrenals are specifically involved and as they are the seat of energy in the physical body this can cause a little fatigue. They are dislodging old fears and anxieties so you should come back better than ever. You may have no reaction and that is fine also. Just make sure you drink plenty of water; coconut water is amazing at hydrating the body as is aloe vera.

Shakti

Shakti is the goddess of kundalini awakening. She encourages self protection and regular chakra balancing meditations to keep one's energy healthy and strong. Loving safe sex is also one her domains. Her male counterpart is Shiva, their balance within us creates the power of kundalini energy and it mirrors our perfect male/female balance. This fusion within us is the fuelling force that organically ignites our kundalini energy that then brings our wholeness into perfect alignment.

This is Shiva's mantra to activate your kundalini alignment.

"Om Namah Shivaya"

(Om Nah-Mah Shee-Vah-Yah)

(Om and salutations, may the elements of this creation abide in me in full manifestation.)

This mantra will balance all the elements in your body, bringing everything into harmony with the mind, body, spirit connection. This then aligns the chakras and instigates kundalini health and energy.

Summary

This layer of the DNA Light Codes represents the chemistry you can see. It receives and transmits, taking the information from the multi dimensional layers and implementing them upon your gene structure. This is where the affirmations, prayers, healing and special foods get processed and programmed into your evolving DNA. Basically, it is central to how everything else works.

Understanding this will help one to understand the mechanics of positive affirmations, repeating sacred mantras, crystal vibrations, scent and singing positive and powerful songs. Anything you deliver to yourself in a strong and empowered way can and will imprint on the cells of your body. Unfortunately even powerful negative emotional experiences do. Drama, pain and loss occur, especially in our times, but that can happen to break down the old cycles of genetic imprinting, now we are reprogramming our cells with new and dynamic ways of thinking and behaving. In doing this we are literally regrowing ourselves and future generations. We are all connected; as we grow we impact the world around us. We especially affect anyone with related DNA, like family. Consider this - you may have family dating back hundreds of years who you have never met, maybe they live in some sad and poverty ridden place in the world. Each time you improve yourself you give them the opportunity to do so also. As your DNA shape shifts, theirs will be affected. Don't ask me how but it has been proven. Read some of Greg Braden's work - he has all the scientific data happening. All is possible and it can be fun. Be happy, feel joy, laugh as often as possible, love, love and love even more, LOVE is the key to healing yourself.

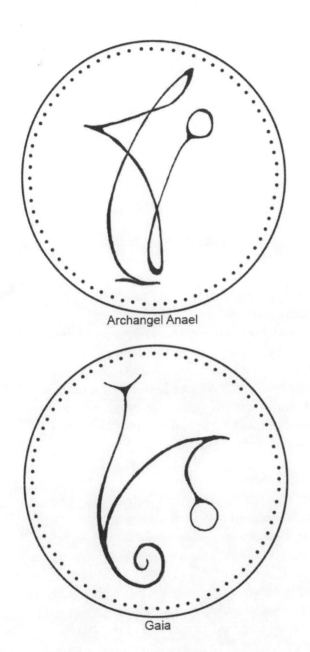

Chapter 3

Sacral Chakra

3rd and 4th Light Codes

Water element

Archangel Haniel

Associated parts of the body: genitals, uterus, large intestine, bowel, bladder, pelvis, lower vertebrae, hip area.

The sacral chakra is located below the naval; it vibrates to a vibrant orange ray. This chakra is the creative chakra, the emotional aspect of our sexuality, intuition and goddess energy. Nurturing the self and connecting to your heart is very much a part of what keeps this chakra healthy. Male and female unity comes together here giving your creative energy so much more power. This is why tantric practices have become so talked about, it weaves these two polarities together in a conscious, and heart centred way. Practicing this with a partner is wonderful but this unity can happen just within the self. There is a tremendous amount of energy stored in this chakra and it is probably one of the most unbalanced chakras most people have.

All these emotions swirl around in here; most of the hundreds of varieties could probably be thinned back to a base of fear. Once the male/female unity within happens such a surge of power is realised and that in itself causes fear, deep soul fear of loss of control. So a gentle approach is always desirable.

For women, hormonal imbalance is a common issue here. This chakras element is water and we are made up of 90% water, all our emotions get imprinted into the holy waters of our being, this is why living as clean and joy-full life as possible is so important. Loving, grateful thoughts are so vital to our healing and well being. If a situation is too hard either surrender or move on, no one expects us to super humanise ourselves - well not just yet. The waters of your body are vital to your well being, your lymphatic system and hormonal system keep your body cleansed and lubricated. Your endocrine system carries the electrical charge of spirit into the physical, if it is not functioning well chaos can result, effecting your health and general well being. This is why our relationships have been so intense for this generation; it is a fast track way to sort out those deep unconscious programs that may be jamming up the well spring of our divine goddess essence. PMT is really just unresolved junk jamming up the flow of your goddess tide; it is a wonderful yardstick on how well you are doing with your emotional well being. Ovarian cysts are like pain surrounding your divine creative expression, abuse and neglect of your pure essence. Love them, bless them and then move on into brighter more harmonious pastures.

Positive Sacral Energy: trusting, expressive, creative, comfortable with ones emotional feelings

Unbalanced: over sensitive, hard on self, feels guilty for no reason, low sexual energy/sex addict, manipulative, fanatical.

Light Codes 3 and 4

The 3rd and 4th Light Codes work to deeply heal our ability to receive love, to actualise a sense of self love with in us. Working with these codes will cause a flushing out of old programs and genetic imprints that stand in the way of truly embracing ourselves on every level and in every cell of our body. Lack of self love is probably one of the biggest core issues of all time, so be prepared to work with this one from time to time, use as needed to reinstate self acceptance during all the kinds of challenges we meet on this journey. As every Light Code and DNA lives within every particle of everything within us and around us you get the understanding that every thing effects everything, nothing is separated, so as we bring them all back into healthy alignment there is a moment of true activation where a synergy of totality occurs linking you rightfully back into the nexus of your truth. Then you become the co-creator you were born to be.

Archangel Haniel

Haniel works with the moon energy, the ruler of our emotional tides. She is a rather beautiful being and relates to goddess energy very well. Haniel means grace, harmony and balance. This angel will get the creative waters of your divine expression flowing for you, she will align your chakra with truth assisting you to see where emotional illusions maybe distorting your field of vision. The sacral chakra is connected to the ethereal level of your light field; this auric layer is the most prone to emotional distortion which can cause self doubt and confusion. Confusion can lead us way off track if we are not careful, loosing ourselves in another's picture of reality. That quiet space within is so important here, it will allow you the space to connect with your inner voice and hear the angelic guidance that is always available. Eckhart Tolle is great to listen to if you need help with this.

Haniel will assist with the strengthening of your psychic gifts, being open to receive grace and experience true beauty-within and around you. She connects you to the moon energy which helps with the emotional moods we go through and for healing magic using herbs and natural remedies.

Crystals

Carnelian is a wonderful, rich vibrant orange. She stirs creativity and motivation, linking to your mental body to help in actualising your creativity. Carnelian is good for uplifting the energy of depression, bringing the fire of life back. She promotes health and happy energy, bringing social opportunities together and general vitality to what ever you ask of her. This is a happy stone, drawing abundance and well being into one's life. I feel carnelian is a magician's stone, working when programmed to assist in magical manifestation work.

Moonstone is a milky variety and is found in cream or slightly apricot hues. She works to balance hormones and all things related to the waters of your body. One's beauty is enhanced by this stone; she brings a translucency to one's skin. Intimacy issues are addressed as well as sexuality and healing of such issues. Calm waters are restored and psychic visions are enhanced. This is an ultimate female crystal, very Goddessy and angelic in its nature.

Pearls and Mother-of-Pearl are two wonders of the water that work well with this watery chakra. The pearl eases irritation, she is smooth and soft, alleviating stress and water retention. She helps us to be comfortable with our emotions. Mother-of-pearl has the most amazing ethereal colours swirling through her; these colours can align your ethereal body with your highest expression of this chakra. The watery nature of this shell assists you to move fluidly with your most feminine energy, engaging with it in a very sensual way. She attracts beautiful angelic energy into your sacred space, assisting you to manifest your highest ideals. She is so gorgeous that she enhances every aspect of your personal beauty. They both lift this chakra into the higher aspects of your spiritual body, thus drawing down your ethereal light and inspiring new and wonderful ways of expressing yourself. They are also good for boosting fertility and assisting a high soul to incarnate.

Crocite is a power house of a crystal. Not that easy to find as it is very fragile and not one to make a direct elixir from. It is a very intense orange colour and boosts the sexual energy way out there. Crocite is probably one of the strongest sexual boosts in the crystal world. She is a wonderful tonic for the sacral chakra, boosting all systems but only as a layout crystal. This crystal is mostly found in Australia.

Aquamarine is usually found in the upper chakras but I shall also include her here as she is so watery in nature. I find she cleanses and renews my hydration when I am feeling overloaded or dehydrated. She is brilliant at bringing the watery emotions back to clear after a healing or difficult time. Added to a crystal elixir for this chakra she will help the other absorb more easily into the cells of your body, flushing the old and protecting the new.

Aquamarine is like a beautiful goddess of the water realm.

Flower Essence for the Sacral Chakra

Mango

Mango is a very Lemurian essence; in fact I feel this chakra and the corresponding Light Codes hold a lot of our Lemurian memories; memories of times when goddess energy was so much more abundant and honoured. The goddess was at the heart of everything we did and the earth was honoured and nurtured from this space. Creativity and sexuality were sacred expressions of our divinity and every one was equal. I feel my essence making skills and knowledge come from my memories of this time and it was something I did often. Mango was a sacred fruit and her energy could heal and lubricate our bodies, assisting them to evolve and stay vibrantly alive.

Her essence carries these memories for me, of verdant plant life, of dolphins and mermaids, crystal energies and angelic light. We had ways of continually staying attuned to the forces of Light and working them into our everyday lives, co-creating with the creator. Healthy, loving sensual experiences wake up this chakra and release our creative codes, bringing the yin and yang of our duality into oneness which activates our sacred memories, getting them flowing and full of new ideas. One does not need a partner for this but it can help.

Mango Essence

Unblocks creative energy, heightening one's senses and connects it to the third eye.

Brings one into the present moment, healing old wounds like emotional anaesthetic, nourishing the endocrine system and bringing back laughter and joy.

Very strengthening on all levels, a tonic for depression and blood sugar stabiliser.

Moisturising your body internally and externally, great for menopausal woman as it keeps those inner lubricants flowing.

Enhances sexual arousal.

Good conception tonic prepares a woman's body, increasing her fertility and assists the incarnating spirit to settle in.

Another essence I use here is Orange Grevillea. I actually use her at the Hara Chakra which is directly linked to the sacral but is the Chinese version of it. The Chinese system feels this hara point to be our source of pure prana and life-force. It is very close to the navel and is a powerful acupuncture point. This point is where I access any old cords that are hooked into the emotional body and powerhouse. These hooks may have come into this life with us, travelling through time and space or been picked up from anyone having some issue with us - even a loved one. What these hooks do is drain our energy and effectively confuse our emotional response to situations. The old emotional vampire situation! This point can need continual clearing and maintenance, particularly when you work in some sort of care industry. I work with AA Michael when using this essence as his cord cutting skills are exemplary.

Essence Information

Works with hara chakra as an emotional detox and healing essence.

Clears and heals attachments, cords and emotional hooks from Hara and energy field.

Heals psychic wounds, opening them up to clear trapped dark energy, parasites and attacks.

Reaches into your holographic blueprint and retrieves lost soul fragments.

Strengthens the will to live, drawing healthy earth energy up to vitalise one and anchor the lower chakras to hold the light body firmly in place.

Great for healers of any kind as it grounds and supports your energy, clearing clients' energy as you go.

Essential Oils for the Sacral

Clary Sage works well for the sacral and solar chakras. She is an antidepressant which offers support during emotionally taxing times or when hormones are running rampant. It actually offers hormonal support; it is a uterine tonic and acts as an aphrodisiac. The effect can be slightly sedative and has been known to induce a euphoric state, which also assists the higher chakras. It seems this oil is an all over assistant in wellbeing. Can cause blood pressure to drop slightly so treat with care.

Sometimes we need a buffer against continual emotional and stressful energy, as these feelings are repressing rather than expanding to your Light Codes and health levels. Oils like clary sage can offer that support.

Jasmine is used as an aphrodisiac and general goddess essence. She enhances all things female, giving a glow to the user. Jasmine creates a calming effect on the emotions and anchors in a lovely light. Jasmine knows her worth and radiates beauty so she will assist you to stay true to your own heavenly light.

Ylang Ylang is another great hormonal assistant, giving energy to the vital adrenals which also offers menopausal support when the adrenals suddenly have twice the work to do. While she assists irritability and nervous tension she can also lower blood pressure. This oil is another aphrodisiac and relaxant, her aroma is intoxicating and should be used gently.

Orange is vitalising, offering her warm and sunny energy to all blends and situations. Energy oozes from her scent, lifting depression and giving the nervous system some bright support. There is digestive support with this oil so if things are a bit sluggish add this lovely to your blend. Orange is great for alleviating depression and picking up energy after flu or other illness. This oil zings through the channels of the body clearing all kinds of malingerers. Bitter Orange is awesome as well; I like it better myself - even zingier!

Vanilla is warming, strengthening and grounding. Not anchoring like the base oils but somehow smooths away any emotional overload that may have been around. She makes things feel warm and safe, nurturing the spirit and bringing back a sense of comfort and peace. It is as if she gently opens the doors of the spirit allowing the healing and time out you need. She is also known for her sensual and attraction blessings.

Rose Geranium is a beautiful, feminine and hormonal balancer; she offers emotional protection and ethereal balance. Geranium is an amazing Earth Goddess energy; she reaches her hand out and offers support at every level to assist you to function at your feminine best.

All these oils help you to stay in a higher state of wellbeing; they raise your vibration, effectively repelling any darker or negative energy from interfering with you. Their lovely energy strengthens your aura giving strength to you when feeling vulnerable. This is so valuable here as almost everyone is rebalancing their emotions and relationship to life, a little protection during these times is a valuable resource.

Ritual of Activation for Sacral Chakra and Light Codes 3 and 4

An orange candle dressed in chosen essential oil

A misting spray of chosen oil in water to clear the space; rose geranium and clary sage would make an ideal combination for this work, (water cleansing corresponds well to this chakra ritual but sage smudge is always fine, if in doubt).

Chosen crystal for this healing and activation.

Take a couple of flower essence drops or place on chakra or place some in the misting bottle.

Say the prayer of protection.

Take some nice deep breaths, breathing into your pelvis, feeling it fill with air, then gently allow the breath to release, feeling all the tension in your body leave, all the tension in your pelvis melting away. Do at least three of these deep breaths.

Invoke Archangel Haniel by saying

"In the name of all that is of the Light, I ask my guides, celestial helpers and Archangel Haniel to please activate, heal and balance my sacral chakra, placing within it the crystalline structures and sacred geometry I need to fully bring my sacral chakra into its highest vibration and health activation. I ask that the corresponding Light Codes 3 and 4 and DNA be brought into perfect harmony with my soul's highest expression now. I command the activation of the 3rd and 4th Light Codes now, bringing them into their highest level of presence. I ask for this healing in all time and space, past, present and future, clearing all past limitations and illusions, bringing me into the present moment. I command this healing to occur on every level of my physical and light bodies, healing at the deepest levels of my cellular make-up, in a loving and gentle way. I now activate my full spectrum of creative energy. I am so grateful for this healing. Thank you. Om Mani Padme Hum."

Be still, see the vibrant orange energy growing stronger in your sacral centre; it is spreading its luminescent light all through your body, attuning each of your Light Codes to their highest expression of the creative 3rd and 4th levels. Relax and feel the guides and angels doing their work, feeling safe and nurtured to become fully realised in your creative fullness.

Write any insights down when you are done, drink plenty of water and do something fun to anchor this new and vibrant energy into your physical life.

Drink carnelian charged water to support the uptake of this new energy.

Remember to safely extinguish candle.

The seed sound for this chakra is Vam (Vahm)

Chanting this sound will bring this centre into balance

Animal Totem

An animal totem for this centre would be the dolphin. Dolphins exude joy and freedom; they love openly within their pods and are quite sensual creatures. They are uninhibited in their joyous leaping and swift movement. The sounds they make are so powerful they have been known to create profound healing in humans, even unborn babies will respond to them. They have been known to communicate with man, aboriginals in more ancient times would communicate with them and the dolphins would round up the fish and herd them in so the tribe could catch their dinner.

When in meditation ask the dolphin energy to come and give you a healing, see yourself lying on a golden sandy beach or in a crystal temple, this creates a space for them to connect with you. It is very gentle and yet quite starry and cosmic, for they are believed to be intergalactic travellers, originating on the star system Sirius. Hold an aquamarine or clear quartz to work with them.

There are many CDs with dolphin sounds blended into the music which work beautifully to enhance this healing. CDs with water sounds are also great as the water works to settle your watery ethereal body, cleansing and calming your emotions.

Goddess Work

Mermaids, Yemaya and Lakshmi all have a place here.

These Light Codes hold so much Divine feminine energy, mysterious and magical, lost but now ready to be reignited and made fertile again.

Who has not felt the watery, sensual inner mermaid at times? She awakens some ancient and mythical part of us that wants to feel this flowingly beautiful energy again.

Go to the ocean or a waterfall, feel the water on your skin, so cool and cleansing. Fresh water is very hydrating and softening, soaking into the pores of your skin and awakening a deep calling. Feel the water cleansing each of your chakras, even if you do this under the shower if no waterfall is available. Breathe the water through each chakra, front and back, cleansing and cooling, washing away the old and leaving a sparkle of rainbow lights in place.

The ocean is deeply cleansing, even being near the ocean sends out tons of negative ions that literally cleanse and charge your aura with positive energy. Sit in a rock pool, let your inner mermaid luxuriate and enjoy this oceanic gift.

Find a shell that holds the sound of the ocean within her, hold her to your ear and feel the peace and connection to the great mother ocean. Keep the shell on your altar, if it is big enough, fill her with water and crystal essence and pour the water over your head, feeling the healing ocean rushing through you, vitalising your emotional body with bright, purified water.

This can also be a healing for the ocean and other water bodies which are continually struggling with pollutions. Fill the shell with water infused with a vibrational essence and hold it close, saying a prayer of healing, then let it flow from the shell into the water. See a stream of light infused water flowing out and sending positive healing energy around the planet. The sirens of the sea and the water Undines (water elementals) will carry your sacred offering and spread it far and wide.

Yemaya

Yemaya is known as the mother of the ocean, the water is her living body. She is always seen as a very beautiful woman, irresistible in her allure and sensuality. Her origins are African and her story spread to the Caribbean and South America. Yemaya works with the moon and female cycles. She is able to see into dreams and can help in releasing you from old programs and destructive or out worn situations.

Make a sea salt bath/foot bath infusion to cleanse and move old stuck energy.

Blend together:

Handful of sea salt and/or Epsom salts

Peppermint and lemon oil for cleansing or ylang ylang and jasmine for sensuality

Mango and or Golden Grevillea essence

A moonstone or moonstone essence

A sprinkling of kelp for nourishing all systems

Some base oil like olive, sesame or almond for moisturising

Light a candle and some incense to lift energy and create a sacred space

Create an intention about why and what it is you are cleansing or creating

Pour the mixture into your bath or foot bath

Say:

"I call upon beloved Yemaya

Goddess of the cleansing waters

Bless my bath with healing light

That I may rise glowing and bright

Blessed Be."

Relax and enjoy a long soak, drink plenty of water to assist the cleansing action and to rehydrate. Feel all your concerns dissolving in your magically charged bath, feel the light infusing every cell of your body with new health and well being, displacing old problems, toxins and emotional pain.

Thank Yemaya and emerge from your bath a glowing and beautiful new you.

Lakshmi

I am including an extra goddess here as some doorways have several functions, especially the lower ones.

Lakshmi is a Hindu goddess of prosperity; she embodies all that is abundant and wonderful about being alive. I always see her surrounded in an amazing golden, apricot, golden light, just glowing with life and absolute beauty. Her symbols are a lotus, conch shell and elephants blowing water around her, all very sacral symbols. The lotus symbolises growing from the mud up into the light, blossoming as one of the loveliest of flowers, this is one of our most sacred symbols of meditation and growth.

All our chakras are evolving, as they lift in frequency, as our Light Codes switch back on, we may find the colours of the chakras change, lifting their hue to higher and lighter shades, the lotus symbolises this in her journey through the watery depths of the mud (our heavier emotions) and raising herself up into the light of her own glory.

Mantra

When we chant mantras, we are embodying and imprinting ourselves directly with divine attributes. The seed sounds assist our chakras to flower open, allowing them to align with our perfected self. Our chakra petals may have closed or become damaged so do not operate in a clear manner. They tend to operate in the way we have been programmed by life to think. So the mantras work to heal the damage and correct their operation. Sound is a powerful and penetrative energy that can re-imprint a more positive message. The goddess mantras are effective as they access a divine blueprint of perfected feminine force. This force can activate within us and greatly assist our power to heal and evolve. My experiences have been wonderful, I have tried and tested them out and find them to be an amazing tool in my self healing.

Ritual of Plenty

Lakshmi's mantra is *"Om Shreem Maha Lakshmiyei Swaha"*

(Om Shreem Lahk-shmee-yea Shah-ha)

Translates as "Om and salutations to She who provides abundance."

Light a candle - orange would be lovely - draw her sigil on the candle

Place some lotus oil, basil (Lakshmi's sacred oil) or one that is listed, on the candle

Scatter some coins around the candle

Bring in a meditative state, using your breath to release any stress

Hold your hands in a receptive cup position, little fingers and outside palms resting together

Visualise your desire for abundance, in what ever form that takes - money for bills, a new dress, creative energy or just to feel overflowing with joy

Chant Lakshmi's mantra

See all your needs being taken care of, golden coins, gems, fruit and light filling and overflowing out of your cupped hands, abundance flowing all around you.

Take some time to sit with this, gentling back into a quiet meditative state, feeling the divine presence of goddess abundance surrounding and filling your life.

Always be grateful

Either snuff the candle out or leave it to burn in a safe and protected space

Place some of the blessed coins in a charity box to spread the abundance

Abundance Spell

Lakshmi's sigil on a small piece of paper

Basil seed or seedling

Pot of soil

A coin

Place some soil in the plant pot, and then place the paper with the sigil on it. Put the basil seedling in the pot and fill with remainder of soil. Place the coin just under the top soil. Hold your pot and chant Lakshmi's mantra, seeing what it is you are wishing to manifest. Hold the vision. If it is money, concentrate on an exact amount and how it will be used.

Add the leaves to your meals and know you are ingesting the goddess's blessings.

The sigil will dissolve into the soil, feeding your plant with multiple blessings.

Leave the pot and give the basil some time to grow. Water it regularly, blessing the water as you feed it. After some time remove the coin and place it in a charity box somewhere, a blessed coin that goes forth to assist others needs to be met.

Summary of Light Codes 3 and 4

Light Codes 3 and 4 are the divine blueprint of duality. It is here that we establish who we are, not what others have imprinted us to believe about ourselves. We establish personal boundaries so we recognise our emotional response to others. It is here that empaths have to learn how to strengthen their auras and learn to distinguish their feelings from that of another's, disconnecting from emotional manipulation and cording. This layer gives us a sense of purpose and direction. Much of the emotional imprinting is found here, past and present. What can also be found here are the tools to heal and become emotionally intelligent. You will find each layer supports all the others, providing the tools, knowledge and divine inspiration to enable one to heal and evolve. As we awaken, all systems start to support you in a whole new way. We hold in our cells the knowledge and ancient memories of all we need.

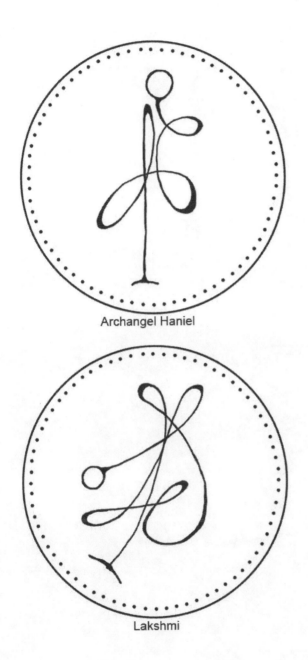

Archangel Haniel

Lakshmi

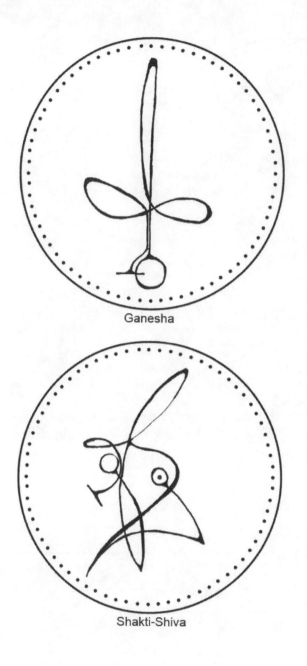

Chapter 4

Solar Plexus Chakra

Light Code 5

Fire Element

Archangel Jophiel

Associated parts of the body; adrenal glands, stomach, upper intestines, pancreas, liver, gall bladder, middle spine.

The solar plexus chakra is situated between your heart and navel. There are so many different opinions on the location but I usually place my crystals over the stomach region if working on the solar plexus. This centre has only one Light Code but it is a powerful one, putting order into our potential chaotic self definition.

This is the point of bright golden sunshine, where the sun shines and lights up our life. When the sun goes down so do we, our health may suffer, depression and low self esteem eventuate. Digestion issues, Candida, weight issues and low energy are also symptoms of imbalance. Healthy self confidence is so important; it generates energy and magnetic manifestation abilities. This sunshine literally fuels one's goals and infuses pure will and drive into one's instincts and decision making. The mind is clear, knowing and trusting the process of one's life and self doubt does not exist. A clear mind creates clear boundaries, the ability to say "no", to know when someone is asking too much or trespassing in one's personal space are very valuable traits to develop here. Clear boundaries keeps one's aura clear, no processing another's issues or wondering if you made the right decision or not. No leaking energy caused by self doubt or low self esteem, which can lead to health issues.

This really is a centre of powerful emotions, deep and impacting and as such deserves to be maintained with care. This chakra is a centre of deep release, when we are processing this is the doorway to clear the old. I is often called the emotional vomit chakra, yucky but quite true. Our ego has a strong hold in this chakra; how we see ourselves, how we want others to see us, how powerful are we, I want to control this so I feel in control, I want to be seen as more advanced than her and on it goes. All very human feelings but they no longer have a place in our evolving lives. You can feel the cords of others when they try to pull you into their power/control games. These cords can influence you and coerce you into behaviour that later on causes you to wonder what just happened, that was not how I am. When we truly know ourselves, love ourselves and respect who we are, others cannot successfully pull you in or psychically challenge you anymore. As you grow you will find others threatened by your growth and there will be other challenges, this is your moment to recognise the end of the old way and consciously step beyond old behaviours, freeing yourself to grow and expand.

Good self esteem is the building block of a healthy and whole human. It literally acts as a compass, guiding you through the many illusions that can trap you and drag you back down and round and round, losing energy and fuelling someone else's story. Do you have a negative inner voice, a self saboteur? This negative inner voice can talk you out of following your dreams, feeling guilty about taking a chance because what if? Spend time getting to know who you really are, delete all the old negative childhood programming and make space for alone time - best investment ever. Doing this will allow you to learn how to truly hear your inner voice of truth, intuition and guidance. Social and urban programming can really have a strong effect on one's self esteem, mass belief systems saying this is what a successful life should look like, bah humbug anyone who tries to break free and be unusually independent or creatively eccentric, this is your life and by taking risks we break down the old conditioning that keeps us locked in old genetic and social programming. This is how we break down the crystallised blocks to our full DNA activation, do the processes and live a life worth living, not controlled by old outdated limitations. If your heart and gut are saying 'Yes, I want this but . . .' ignore the 'but' and explore how it can be achieved, set goals (very solar plexus activity) write out achievable steps, do a ritual of clearing and visioning of your outcome, or simply just go for it. The universe will support what ever your dreams are calling in, the universe loves change, just step back and let her set the wheels in motion.

This centre of Light Codes requires you to believe in yourself. It matters not what others think. If you allow others to undermine your self-belief they are undermining your power on a deep level, even cellular, and no one has that right. What you do is between you and spirit, your personal truth is about being in alignment with your own integrity and always doing your best. Someone in their power operates this way, they hold their own energy, they believe in themselves and their choices, they become a leader in their own life. All this generates strong energy in the body, digestion and nervous system operate well. Healthy, optimistic energy generates healthy cellular turn over and an ability to move forward and evolve. When this Light Code is strong and healthy it supports the network of your system to hold its own. It is like an anchoring of your ego but in a way that is in balance and supports your wholeness to reconnect and function safely, in alignment with your spirit and the greater whole. You are empowered to safely lead and empower others, giving expression to your greater connection and truth.

Light Code 5

This is where we let go of the ego and merge with the divine will. We become one with higher guidance and knowing. Our mental body and will are integral to the healthy operating and evolvement of the 5th Light Code. We need the ego as it keeps us grounded and operating as an individual on the earth plane. Without some healthy ego, it would be very hard to maintain boundaries and have a clear sense of self. As we ascend up the spiral we learn to release fear which is negative ego and merge back into the one heart. We become that co-creator learning to operate from our higher knowing, not our fears and limitations, which can be hardwired into our DNA coding. As all the parts of our spiral are actually operating as one and yet as separate chakra doorways it makes it easy to address the issues that come up for us. I love that the Earth Star is operating within the solar plexus to ground our divine will.

This Light Code can be quite affected from past lives (as they all can) because the use of power has been a fairly intense learning curve. Apart from power over others being a big one, many of the past disasters of the earth have been due to not listening to the divine directives of the creator but taking the role of power hungry creator into their own hands and causing some major blunders ... Bermuda Triangle, Noah's flood. Then imagine the aftershock upon looking back once in spirit and seeing the results of your ideas and ego based impulses. The group grief of the fall of Atlantis is a major curve of healing at this time. Many are gathering in communities to support this healing and recreate through group memory a similar sense of group harmony and a spiritually based life. Our group memories are supporting each other to remember.

Archangel Jophiel

Archangel Jophiel brings in the bright yellow ray, bringing sunshine right into our aura. This is a beautifully positive angel, bringing joy and creative solutions, allowing one to find the path of least resistance to one's desired outcome. Joy is Jophiel's tune – let us bring joy to all that we do, if joy does not resonate with your actions then maybe think again about your direction. It is told in a myth that Jophiel created the citrine crystal as a calling stone for the force of Liberation. Liberation is freedom from the ego and a reconnection to the freedom of the spirit and souls flight. Jophiel's citrine ray is a ray of sunshine, dispelling our self doubts and pessimistic thoughts. This crystal ray connects the solar plexus to the crown chakra opening a connection of divine will, inspiration flowing through to action and manifestation.

Jophiel is known as a wise angel. He connects one to their higher self and all knowingness. There is a connection made with the masters and other angels. He works like a bridge between the worlds, assisting the co-creative process, connecting us to source and pure states of consciousness. He brings us back into the rays of pure sunshine, healing the damage of old doubts or present problems. His ray can light up our path forward, burning away any negatives littering the way. From his position of light he sees all things and knows the outcome you desire, his light will then liberate your karma and show you the way. Spirit truly wants us to be happy and back in tune with our highest expressions, we just have to invoke their aid then let them in. Creative solutions to big and small issues that arise in our lives are Jophiel's specialty.

Allow his rays of sunshine show you the way.

Crystals

Citrine is such a positive crystal that it never needs cleansing. I probably still would but because of this it is the ultimate solar plexus crystal. The sunshine energy brings instant healing and upliftment to the potential issues of poor self esteem and powerless feelings the solar plexus can hold. These issues can cause poor digestion, toxins and emotional turmoil. Citrine assists a return to balance and detoxification; used with Jophiel's energy citrine makes a potent healing tool.

She offers purification on all levels, assists in manifesting wealth and abundance, brings healthy, positive energy into your life, shifts old patterns of negativity and brings back the magic.

Amber is another brilliant sunshine healing tool. It is actually tree resin, solidified from ancient trees. Amber is very protective; it carries the energy of the tree so its energy is strong and resilient. It is very calming and grounding so allows the mind to see more clearly. She also has antiseptic qualities which will cleanse the bodies systems of toxins and parasites – yes, even human ones. Amber helps dissolve old patterns from the past that are handed down through DNA. This is a great stone for healers to wear as she offers a gentle but effective shield of protection, grounding and clearing the energy as the healing takes place.

Tigers Eye brings courage and calm to one's power centre. It goes in and sorts out the confusion that can often cloud this chakra. Fears, negativity and introversion will fade, clearing the way for intuitive solutions and abundant new ideas. She is quite grounding and enhances the growth of abundance and well being in one's life. The lovely way the colours and light shift through the crystal are its ability to shift one's mind set and alter realities.

Golden Calcite is very calming; she banishes self doubt and nourishes the endocrine system. Calcite assists with past life recall, when we recall past memories it helps with the dispersal of its karmic imprint. Calcite helps these past memories dissolve back into the light.

Malachite is green and green contains a lot of yellow so she imparts a healing that unites the heart and solar plexus, bringing the heart's action back into the seat of power. Malachite can shield us from many of life's negatives. She draws in life's sweetness and eases the often deep concerns we carry in our solar plexus. Because of its ability to draw in the sweetness she assists with the healing of diabetes. Diabetes stems from the pancreas and our inability to process sugars, the sweetness life has to offer. Allow malachite to dissolve this energetic imprint and use it to program healthy and abundant goals into your life. Malachite can be used at the heart as well.

Peridot is another green stone that carries a lot of yellow, healing those programs/emotions that can stem from our self esteem and cause a blockage in our hearts. This kind of blockage can sabotage our ability to receive love and abundance flowing into our lives. She gently heals anger and jealousy which can result from blocked emotions and diminished ability to receive joy.

Peridot works closely with the fairy/elemental kingdom, inviting magic to come and enchant our lives. She draws all things good towards us, healing our belief in the goodness of life. This crystal is very good for digestive issues and balancing our ability to receive our inner nourishment.

Flower Essence for the Solar Plexus Chakra

Golden Wattle

What could be more appropriate for our sunshine chakra than golden wattle. The warm honey scent and golden light it gives off are so healing and uplifting, leaving no room for heavy emotions and low energy.

Works to balance the solar plexus energy

Energises and brightens one's outlook on life

Warms our centre with pure sunlight, stimulating the digestive system and lifting the vibration of our inner power

Assists with the healing of Candida, depression and fatigue

Bolsters self confidence, assists one to deal positively with situations that no longer serve one's highest good. The brightness of this essence illuminates what needs to be cleared and shines a light on the new direction to take

Old negative situations start to drop away

Assists the healing of nervousness and anxiety, giving you back your inner authority

She opens the door between the worlds so access is made for guidance and healing

Chamomile is another great flower essence for the solar plexus.

Chamomile will bring calm when everything is moving quickly

and emotional overwhelm threatens.

Brings healing to grief and an ability to cope, like an emotional anaesthetic

She declutters the mind, bringing clarity and clear vision, allowing for an unemotional response to choice making

Camomile provides relief for digestive disturbances

Essential Oils for Solar Plexus Support

Lemon, bright, citrusy lemon works wonders on the digestive system. The oil is extracted from the fruit peel. The scent is immediately clearing, like an antiseptic to the body in all systems. The mind clears, the aura brightens and the tummy, especially the liver, calm and settle. Using lemon topically will stimulate the immune system, rebuilding cellular integrity and health. Lemon alkalises your system and detoxs the lymphatics. She provides a protection from viruses and negative energy from others.

Bergamot is another sunshine oil. She dispels depression, lifts one's energy to allow a lighter view of life. Bergamot moves stagnant energy, mind, body and spirit. Once this qi is moving again our health and vitality can return. She moves and redirects one's energy into a healthy direction, great for breaking addictions. A handy hint: place a drop in the palm of your left hand to draw prosperity into your life.

Fennel is a very soothing oil. Placed on the soles of the feet, fennel will calm an over active digestive system, remove toxins and relieve nausea.

Ginger is a very warming oil, dispelling any damp and congestion in the digestion and kidney area. Ginger improves one's kidney energy thus boosting libido and life force energy. This is yang oil which improves one's will to do and achieve, to see projects through and fire up the system.

Cinnamon is another wonderful, warming oil. Never use undiluted as it is quite caustic. Cinnamon also balances blood sugar and is wonderful for people who have diabetic tendencies.

Peppermint is such an all round amazing oil. A drop or two of peppermint will clear and uplift any space. Used diluted on the back of the neck will cool an over heating body, soothe headaches and settle one's digestive system. She just infuses anything with instant cleansing and clearing. The air around her clears and the mind can see clearly again, confusion, doubt and manipulation all dissolve away. Peppermint is great oil for floor washes, room spritzer and dispelling negative interference.

Clove. I am including quite a few oils here as this centre is so connected to digestion and core health. Clove is an oil that stimulates digestion, helps heal and clear candida and works to relax muscles and relieve arthritic conditions. She works on subtle levels also to cleanse the light body. Place a couple of whole clove buds in a cup of green tea with a squirt of lemon juice and you have a wonderfully cleansing and uplifting tea.

Ritual for Activation and Healing of Solar Plexus and Light Code 5

A yellow candle

Sage smudge or lemon spritz

Essential oil to dress candle and anoint body

Jophiel's sigil engraved on candle or placed on your body

Chosen crystal

Place candle on a safe burning plate and light

Have crystal in front of candle or placed on body

Say prayer of protection

Cleanse yourself and room with sage or lemon spritz

Take flower essence if it is available or place on chakra point

Put yourself into a deeply relaxed state

Invoke AA Jophiel by saying:

"In the name love and light I ask my guides, celestial helpers and Archangel Jophiel to please open, activate and balance my solar plexus chakra, placing within it the crystalline structures and sacred geometry I need to fully bring my solar plexus into its highest vibration and health activation. I ask that the corresponding Light Code 5 and DNA be brought into perfect harmony with my soul's highest self expression now. I command the activation of the 5th light Code now, bringing it to its highest level of perfected presence on every level of my light body and beingness in all time and space. I am so grateful for this healing, thank you. Om Mani Padmi Hum."

Sit or lie quietly and allow the healing to take place.

The guides and angels need a little time to do their work.

Breathe into the solar plexus area, see a golden yellow light glowing and filling your whole body. The yellow light lifts and activates your soul's energy, raising your vibration and connecting into your higher self. This movement then draws down your soul's light, travelling down through your crown chakra and healing, activating and connecting you to a higher source of self for renewal. Your higher guides can access your energy through this opening providing deep healing on many levels and rewiring your connection to source.

The seed sound for this centre is Ram (rahm)

A quick way to bring balance is to chant the sound for a few minutes.

Animal Totem

An animal totem for this chakra would be the Ram. The ram climbs steep mountain sides; he uses his will to keep a strong footing and to go where no mere mortal can. His will is strong and able to keep on keeping on. A valuable attribute when life gets a little challenging.

Drinking chai tea is great for this centre. The warm spicy tea will fire up this fire centre, dispelling gloom and the side effects of self doubt.

Keeping the fire of the sun alive here is as important as the sun is to our planet. The fire keeps the engine running, keeps all systems working well, burns up the old when you are finished with it and lights the pathway forward. The burning up of old toxic waste is very important to us on all levels; it keeps the healthy integrity of our cellular make up clear and able to regenerate. You cannot effectively evolve if this old waste builds up, it suffocates the cells and no oxygen or new data can get through to evolve the cell to new levels of ascension. Sometimes 'flu' is a good thing for it gets into you and burns the old away, allowing for a new beginning.

Goddess Work

Brigid

For this doorway we shall work with Brigid. She is an amazing goddess of fire and sunlight, which she displayed through her craft work with iron forging. Brigid also assists us with protection, healing, herbs and creative thought and action. My vision of her is of a very large female spirit, she stands firmly upon the earth, protecting the magic of the earth and all her elementals, she is a warrior goddess as well as an earth mother, protective, healing and nurturing but don't try and fool her for she sees all. Brigid has been called the female equivalent of AA Michael and is fondly called "the bright one".

Sunrise is the perfect time to connect with her. It is here that she offers you the opportunity to start again, to rise fresh and new and see what life has to offer.

Ritual of Purification

Using fire, Brigid will help you to burn away what no longer serves your life's higher purpose.

You will need:

A fire-proof dish

A candle inscribed with Brigid's sigil

Ginger, lemon and peppermint blended in carrier oil to dress candle

Pen and paper

Write on the paper whatever situation you are requiring help with or maybe ready to end and pass on from; this maybe an emotion you wish to heal, a health problem or a personal situation with another. Leave blame behind and focus on a quiet and peaceful resolution.

Light your prepared candle and place in fire-proof dish

Say:

"Brigid Bright

Brigid Light

Please assist me

With my plight."

Feel her Light coming down through you, melting away all worries and concerns. She wraps her mantle of softest blue around you, comforting and warm, fragrant with lavender. Through your heart show her your situation, just for a moment sitting with it, and then become aware of her Light dissolving all trace of it from your heart.

Place the paper in the flame and see it all being purified by fire, by love and the care of the goddess energy.

Then say:

"Brigid of Earth's Divine Power

Bless me in this hour

Bringer of Sun's Light

Protect my health, my wealth and might.

Thank you, sister. Blessed be."

When you feel complete, take the ashes and either let them blow away in the wind or place them under a favourite tree or plant where mother earth can transmute the energy back into healing light.

Solar Plexus Mantra

"Om Ram Ramaya Swaha."

(Om Rahm Rah-mah-yah Swah-ha)

"Om and salutations to that perfection in the physical realm which was Rama, whose attributes exist in me also, kindly manifest."

This mantra warms and empowers the solar centre with positive energy. It liberates us from that which stands in our way. It is a more masculine mantra - Ghandi favoured this mantra.

Layer 5 Conclusion

Layer 5 is the essence of yourself expression and physical divinity, protect and nurture it. This is our divine embodiment, how our spirit expresses itself, balances its power and how we learn and process just what we choose to embody and evolve from. This learning gets processed here and then implemented and imprinted into our evolving self. Much of our learning is an offering from our spirit through the conduit of our sacred Light Codes, an awakening of what our potential seed self already knows and a question: "Are you ready to awaken and become this aspect of your divinity or is your ego still overpowering your ability to move on?" The ego can effectively disable our higher Light Codes and trick us, through habitual thinking, into staying in an old way of behaving. For many it feels very fearful to let go of old programs so they stay where they are, it can feel like a part of you is dying, even though that part is dysfunctional.

It is here we get the opportunity to disable the old crystallised format and upgrade, to engage our mental body to sift through the confusion and come out with a new aspect of self, then using the will, instigate and vigilantly keep focused on the new aspect and eventually weaken the old programs. These programs are hardwired into the brain; we are now creating new neural pathways that will forge a new soul direction. Vigilance is so important - it is like going to the gym to strengthen our muscles. We also need to use our will/mind to strengthen our new resolves for the old will periodically pops back up, teasing and testing you until you have a clear and new resolve and have truly awakened and implemented the new code.

Use your tool box to assist you with this.

Learn to take a cleansing breath when faced with a confusing moment. Confusion is often the old and the new coming face to face for a clearing. A breath allows the mind a moment to disengage with the situation before making a decision based on old habitual thinking.

Protective oils and essences strengthen the light body assisting you to stay in your vibration and not be coerced by another who may not want you to break free of old conditioning.

Take some time to be still, teach the mind to be still. One's own thoughts can then be seen so much more clearly.

Keep grounded in your own reality, not another's.

Check you have no cords attached from another; use AA Michael to assist with cord cutting.

Do a cleansing and grounding exercise, taking a shower before any major decisions are made that you are unsure about.

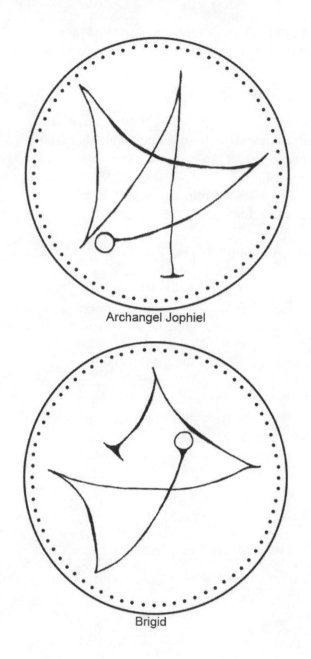

Chapter 5

Heart Chakra - Anahata

Light Codes 6 and 7

The heart chakra is found over the mid chest, between the breasts. There is a physical and spiritual energy found with this centre. The heart is where we step up and start to operate in a higher frequency. This is where we become 'Divine Love', incarnate on the earth plane. The heart chakra rules the heart, thymus gland, lungs, arms, hands, pericardium, and blood pressure. It presents as green but has a rose pink light to it as well; this is the higher heart activation.

We experience sexual love at the sacral centre but at the heart it is stimulated from within; it is a state of being; learning to be in love with yourself rather than depending on another to provide this for you. When we still depend on another as our source of love then that is when all sorts of difficult emotions come into play, muddying up our pure centre of love. The heart chakra is connected with the movement between the physical and non-physical sense of self. Through the compassion and unconditional love of this chakra, we start to open the necessary doors to an expansion of perception. By becoming one with life and all that is, we gain entry into the sacred place of spiritual understanding and a true acceptance of all of who we are as a spiritual being. Developing a compassionate disposition towards situations and our fellow humans is a key to ending the cycles of separation.

Forgiveness is the antidote to most of what may ail the heart and cause physical and energetic blockages here. Sometimes this forgiveness goes back lifetimes, lives lost, betrayed, misunderstood; there is a myriad of potential issues to rebalance and release. As we reclaim a new part of ourselves through the process of soul retrieval and forgiveness, we give our precious immune system a marvellous boost. The immune system is our Holy Grail. It is here that we collect, love and forgive all that has been and transmute it into gold, the gold of ascension.

The Star of David is a sacred geometry symbol that is often used to represent the heart chakra. It has one triangle coming down from heaven, point first and one coming up from the earth, the point entering into the heavenly centre. The two overlap symbolising the union of heaven and earth. They are the sacred marriage of the male and female, a perfect union of masculine and feminine energy, embraced within the one heart. Relationships are such a hotbed of healing as we learn to love our partners and go deeper and deeper with them. Sometimes what we came together with someone to learn has been completed so we move on. Time alone is good as it gives the individual time to integrate the healing of the union. Once that has been accomplished then it is possible to magnetise another into your life to continue the evolvement of the love process. If a true understanding of the learning behind the completion is not received and blame and anger continue then it is probable that the individual will attract the same relationship situation. This is where a nice detailed list of goodies you would like your new partner to embody comes in - but choose wisely with what you ask for. Personally I believe it makes more sense to keep doing self love exercises so that you are overflowing with inner light/love and magnetise someone to you who will love you and respect you for who you are. A true refection of the love you are becoming.

Relationships can push all sorts of buttons, revealing stuff you never knew you still carried within you. The deeper one travels into the heart of love with another, the deeper the healing goes, you feel deeper into the darker recesses of your love and all sorts of feelings can surface. Learn to own these feelings: this does not mean you let another treat you badly but check in to see just what this revelation is trying to show you. Good communication skills are very helpful so that the two can learn to process and grow together rather than get lost in blame, hurt feelings and rejection. Sometimes it is simply a new level of deep love that is triggering a blockage to the furthering of your connection to the divine. Learn to recognise what is simply a pain brought about by deeper states of love and what is maybe the end of a partnership. Emotional pain can be so intense that at times it makes it hard to discern the truth of a situation. For this is the crux of the heart chakras function, to reveal the truth and then carry you into deeper connection with the Divine, your pain is actually your separation from God, your partner is simply mirroring this point of pain back to you so it can be recognised and healed.

So this is where we learn to foster a deep sense of self love and acceptance - warts and all! The Buddha said "First pray for yourself and then pray for others." For me, this is permission to care for myself as much as I do for others. What he is saying is that you are no good as a vessel of universal love if your vessel is empty. We do so much good by being an example of truth and a radiation of love. When we are full then our Light Body radiates universal truth, unconditional love and acceptance into the world around us, touching others as we shop and live our lives. This in itself is true service to the universe.

Signs of imbalance

Obsessive attachments to love, addictive relationship issues, too much empathy and feelings for others, stress, fear of not being lovable, "door mat" types, unforgiving, hay fever, nervous problems, asthma, digestive issues, immune problems, heart problems, endocrine issues, closed and fearful about receiving love or being in love.

Light Codes 6 and 7

I AM Divine Love, learning to bring it back to love, focusing on inner, self aware love. Doing this in all situations is paramount to transforming this vital code, no matter the moment, how challenging it may be, focus on the inner chamber of your heart and radiate this love through out your body. By imprinting this feeling you are blocking any situation from ever robbing you of this divine birthright: to be an expression of and experience of love. This is how we can start the process of becoming Divine

Presence. I am not saying that we have to "love" everything but you are to bring this love into active focus within yourself at every opportunity to negate the potential damage of the challenging forces at work in our world. In doing this you emit a frequency of energy and silent sound that causes a shift in the moment which transmutes the energy of your experience and surroundings. This is how we can begin to imprint reality with new data and cause a groundswell of shift and change. We are lifting the vibrational fields of existence and illusion and shifting them into the next dimension, literally leaving behind the old and dysfunctional programs. By being in our hearts we delete the old and heal our separation. Now we no longer need to be confronted with such chaos, we can co-create our experiences and live a new age. Thus we anchor the six pointed star, living in the centre of a unified field of light.

Through prayer, meditation and soul-full activities we align our Self with our Higher Self and truly start to become our incarnated Higher Self.

Archangel Raphael

AA Raphael comes in on the Emerald Ray. This was the ray Christ used to draw upon in his healing ministrations. The Emerald Ray has the potential to penetrate our bodies on a deep cellular level to bring healing, regeneration and consciousness back into the organism. This is why green foods are so powerfully healing, e.g. spirulina.

Raphael's energy also brings emotional truth to situations that may be the underlying cause of your illness. His energy sweeps in and expands the cellular matrix of congestion, allowing it to breathe again and open back up into a state of integrated health. States of shock, denial and deep grief can be gently healed and tended to by his healing team. Raphael's energy will assist your energy to superimpose itself into situations that will bring to light that which is needed to bring closure to a soul/life lesson, assisting the learning to be integrated and completed. AA Raphael can deeply assist with healing and dissolving the illusions we often base our life on, illusions that are keeping us trapped in our 3D existence. He can liberate our emotions and habitual reactions to outdated scenarios. He brings unity between opposites, unifying the Star of David geometry of our heart chakra. His energy is calming and brings a clear and pure flow directly from source.

Working with his energy also heals the planet, energising the positive elemental beings of the nature world, raising the energy and healing the veils that keep us locked in illusions.

The rosy pink ray also has a part to play in the healing of the heart chakra. This ray penetrates deeply into the core of the heart, opening and healing the spiritual aspect of this chakra. The rosy pink ray dissolves deep hurts that have closed us off to our divine source of love. Our heart is like a rose bud that once she has been given attention starts to open into a fully blown rose, allowing a continual flow of purity to open you up to receive and generate universal love. Self love assists this flower to blossom and it is this healing that allows a relationship based on equality and mutual loving respect to enter one's life. Christ Consciousness is then developed and activated with this level of self awareness.

AA Chamuel is found in the vibration of the pink ray. She can help you to attain this level of self love, bringing healing to your heart and leading towards inner wholeness. Forgiveness of self and others is the key to this ray and its integration into your life. Forgiveness does not mean "what you did to me is ok." What it means is that you are no longer willing to carry the pain of what that situation caused. AA Chamuel when called upon comes in like a pure wave of love, dissolving all blockages to love that the individual is legitimately ready to release.

Heart Chakra Crystals

Green Apophyllite: the sea-foam green clusters of Apophyllite are brilliant healers of the heart. They marry the sensitivity of the heart to the health of the body. Having such a watery nature they are able to truly penetrate the heart and cellular make up of its component in our bodies. The watery nature of this stone is so cleansing to our emotional body, bringing a calming and healing perspective. Apophyllite works very closely with the nature devas and can enhance and balance their light in our personal and planetary consciousness. She also assists with the healing of old karmic wounds, cleansing then healing the scar tissue.

Pink and Green Calcite: any calcite is a very soothing stone. The pink and green variety will work closely with the heart to soothe and heal, assisting with times of transition such as loss or separation.

Emerald is an age-old token of love, her deep green energy penetrating the heart and opening it to receive healing on a deep cellular level. Emerald activates healing gifts and assists us to walk a path of divine love and abundance. This gem has a royal light about her, activating one's own sovereign nature, dispelling any old patterns of self neglect.

Jade is a wonderful all round healing gem. She is affordable and easily found. Her gifts are many, offering healing, abundance and dream time messages. Jade is like the wise old sage, offering solutions to one's questions. Place a piece under your pillow when you are experiencing confusion and allow jade to take you on a dream journey that will bring illumination and clarity. She is calming to those in need of comfort and offers a wonderful healing vibration.

Chrysoprase is an amazing clear green. This stone refreshes, invigorates and renews the heart's energy. She is like a fresh breeze, blowing through and clearing any stagnancy. The green connects you to the earth's heart beat, synchronizing you to the healing forces of the nature kingdom. She can resolve inner conflict and self sacrificing tendencies.

Green Aventurine is the four leaf clover of the crystal kingdom. She opens your heart to receive abundance, healing any resistance to this flow as she works with you. The stone has a sparkle within it that energises your manifestations, employing an earth elemental to assist with your financial endeavours. Her sparkle effervesces her way through your heart, opening and healing any sadness and depression.

Kunzite is a stone of pure love. Think about Mother Mary or Kuan Yin - they both seem to represent the qualities of this precious stone. Humanity has a fair way to go to embody the unconditional love activated by this frequency. She activates the true wisdom of love in the deepest chambers of the heart. A memory is activated of what true love feels like. Kunzite also assists mothers to be able to draw a high soul down the spiral pathway from heaven, enabling them to incarnate more comfortably into the earth plane.

Rhodocrosite links the sacral, heart and crown chakras, taking love and passion into new spiritual heights. She is a wonderful healing stone for women, assisting in the healing of sexual trauma by linking it back into a higher source for healing. There is a very nourishing energy in this stone, healing the layers of grief around our womanhood and gently reopening us to a more unified sense of self.

Rose Quartz can dissolve anger, hurt, jealousy and guilt inspiring forgiveness. Self love is the gift offered by this crystal, deeply cleansing and healing the heart and opening it to a whole new way of experiencing life. It is like looking through a lens of love, as she filters the pain and offers a pure state of love.

Pink Tourmaline links the heart with the crown chakra, taking the heart's energy to a higher vibration. She assists you to see your gifts and offers new visions of how to use them in service to the whole. This can be so essential when one has gone through a lot of deep soul healing and loss; direction can be lost and self esteem shattered. The beautiful pink tourmaline will refresh the soul, infusing a new sense of self and a magnetic quality of attraction but only attracting what is known through the lens of love to be one's true calling.

Flower Essence - Heart Chakra

Peach

Peach was the first essence I made. She just glowed at me one spring morning, fairy energy and angel light shining all around her. Her love was the doorway for my entrance into this magical time of tuning into the deva kingdom to create my essences. The radiating beauty of this being reached into my heart and touched on my loss, my grief and started a healing process of repair and re-opening me to a whole new magical chapter of my life.

Works to heal and open the heart chakra

She is a very ethereal essence, bringing spirit into your physical presence

Stimulates your higher heart energy opening you to joy and abundance

Brings a new level of relating to your relationships, use for activating a tantric flow in your partnership

Assists with conception and pregnancy

Hormonal balancer, switches on your higher DNA codes of sacred feminine/masculine balance, drawing from ancient Lemurian Seed Codes to usher in your true balanced sacred heart power

Activates the etheric body and ethereal fluidium, aligning all the subtle bodies, especially the mental, emotional and soul bodies. It then brings these harmonics into the physical body to assist the healing of mental and emotional diseases.

As it strengthens the ethereal fluidium, it acts as a screen against the sun's ultra-violet rays, giving assistance on a cellular level. This allows us to absorb more cosmic light.

Red Rose

Another wonderful essence for the heart is the Red Rose. This essence was delivered to me by Mary Magdalene, who is in service to assist us to retrieve our true hearts balance with our inner cosmic Christ and sacred marriage.

Provides the passion to keep going when one is worn out from the challenges of life

Reignites passion in committed relationships

Activates one's inner authority

Brings in one's inner goddess, grounds this new awareness of one self

Reconnects one to their inner Christ, opening new fields of awareness and a deeper heart connection to deal with the expansion

Gives the skin a new radiance

Strengthens spleen and heart meridians and the emotional body so one can surrender to love and Christ consciousness, heals the fears which hold us back from embracing our light.

The peach essence is the one I use in my healing work; the rose essence is a master essence connecting us to Mary Magdalene.

Essential Oils for Heart Chakra

Rose Oil opens the heart, like petals opening up to allow the sunlight to dance within again. She warms and nurtures the inner self, allowing a field of light to expand around you, a love that enables the true self to shine through. Passion is awakened, confidence in one self to experience deeper states of love. Rose offers a protection also; her vibration is so high that it effectively shields you against lower thought forms and entities, lifting your heart back up into a more exalted way of being.

Jasmine activates the heart moving it towards greater experiences of love. Jasmine is an aphrodisiac and is used for fertility. She eases depression and stress related conditions. Visualise while smelling the oil how a perfect night with the partner of your dreams might feel and look like. Hold a rose quartz crystal and imbue the crystal with your vision, then place it under your pillow while you sleep.

Jasmine also assists you to connect with your higher heart allowing you to experience your divine connection.

Neroli is another aphrodisiac; she calms nervous tension, allowing you to unfold and melt into the arms of love and bliss. Her sweet intoxicating perfume carries you into the realms of angels and fairies, feeling their magic and love all around you. She will open your arms, your eyes and ultimately your heart to embrace all these magical spaces that we have forgotten in our soul's grief, bringing them back into our reality to create a new way of being.

Yarrow is sweet, protective and healing. She will act as a guardian to the gates of your heart while you heal, filtering out that which would compromise your healing. She will reveal that which no longer serves your higher good and heal and reweave the ethereal light of your aura, healing any holes and wounds, assisting a new wholeness to evolve within you. Yarrow staunches any leaking energy, allowing new levels of vibrant energy to build within you physically and spiritually.

Ritual of Activation for Heart Chakra and Light Codes 6 and 7

A pink or green candle

Sage or frankincense to cleanse and create a sacred space

Chosen essential oil for candle and heart chakra

Heart Chakra Sigil - AA Raphael

Chosen crystal

Heart chakra essence to take or bless chakra with

Optional idea: place chosen heart oil and essence in some water and spritz self and room.

Say prayer of protection

Smudge, incense or spritz room

Place candle in a safe container, sigil may be carved on candle or placed underneath.

Anoint it with chosen oil and light.

Place crystal on self, hold it or place it next to candle.

Take a couple of drops of the essence and place a drop on your heart

Put yourself into a relaxed state, do some deep breathing, calming and clearing all thoughts, bringing yourself into the present moment, feeling all tension leaving your heart, mind and body.

Invoke AA Raphael

"In the name of love and light I ask my guides, celestial helpers and Archangel Raphael to please open, activate and balance my heart chakra, placing within it the crystalline structures and sacred geometry I need to fully bring my heart chakra into its highest vibration and health activation. I ask that the corresponding Light Codes, 6 and 7 and DNA be brought into perfect harmony with my soul's highest expression now. I

command the activation of the 6th and 7th Light Codes now, bringing them into their highest level of presence on every level of my light body and beingness. I am so grateful for this healing. Thank you. Om Mani Padme Hum."

Sit or lie quietly allowing the angels, guides and helpers to assist you to anchor in this healing. Breathe into your heart, feel warmth suffusing you with love. See a rose bud in the centre of your heart, as you breathe in and out the petals of the rose open, just like your heart. You can smell the sweet perfume of a rose; it is completely filling your body, opening the heart/love energy in every cell of your body. The petals are deeply healing your inner heart, allowing the heart's potential to fully flower like the rose. The rose offers a protection as your heart learns to feel safe to be so fully awakened.

Do this meditation and activation as often as needed.

Prayer to invoke Archangel Chamuel

"In the name of love and light I call upon AA Chamuel to fill me with the light of the rosy pink ray. Please assist me with the divine energy of forgiveness and understanding, that I may experience tolerance for myself and others. Please surround me in your mantle of pink light bringing comfort and peace to myself and all concerned. Om Shanti, Shanti, Shanti."

You may like to insert a description of the situation that is troubling you if you feel a need for focused attention on resolution.

The seed sound for the heart chakra is Yam (Yahm)

Chanting this sound will assist with the healing and balancing of this chakra.

Animal Totem

The dove

The dove is the symbol of the goddess Venus, also known as Aphrodite. The dove is a symbol of purity and the pure flight of the soul. Love provides the wings that enable our soul to evolve and ascend to greater heights of awareness. As our love becomes pure we are able to expand our ability as spiritual beings, our empathic psychic nature strengthens and we can explore other realms and "see" truth safely. When we still carry too much baggage and negative emotional conditioning we run the risk of magnetising others' stuff through our empathy. The dove offers a symbol of pure existence, flying above the turmoil of human experience and moving us into an experience of the pure flight of spirit.

Goddess Work

In this section we shall look at the goddess Venus, Mary Magdalene with Radha and Krishna as the divine couple.

Mantra

"Om Mani Padme Hum"

(Om Mah-nee Pahd-mey Hoom)

"The jewel of consciousness is in the heart's lotus."

This is one of the ultimate mantras, for as we integrate all things and become one with our heart and the One Heart then we are truly on our way to spiritual mastery. This is a mantra chanted by masters, to keep their hearts space open and evolving, encompassing ever greater awareness and compassion. Chant this 108 times whenever your heart needs a good workout and to assist in the integration of new levels of evolvement. I use it at the end of many of my prayers and invocations as a way of integrating the energy deep into the gateway of the heart.

Venus/Aphrodite

Venus is the goddess of love; she has her roots in Roman mythology. In Greece she is known as Aphrodite. Their spirit essence is very similar but Aphrodite is probably known for her lustful ways a little more than Venus. Venus is the planet of love which is how this goddess got her name; Aphrodite is an off-shoot of Venus, embodying a more defined understanding of her archetypal role. Aphrodite would link well with the sacral chakra in ritual work for lust, romance and healing of abuse issues. She helps women to feel confident about their sexuality, to enjoy either a moment of lust or a long term relationship, keeping the fire of love alive.

Venus is the planet of vital magnetism, she magnetises her desires, her charisma is strong and her life force is vital and alive. Venus is the enchantress, she entrances what she wants towards her, where as Mars energy goes out and gets what he wants. Working with Heart energy can be very powerful. This is why it is so important to have a clear intention, heal the issues within your heart, so that when you turn that magnetism on only what is healthy for you draws close. The devil card in the tarot is an example of how we can draw unhealthy experiences towards us. Yes, they help us learn but remember to recognise them and do the healing work, do not become addicted to them.

Aphrodite/Venus is the goddess of love, beauty and nature. It is this connection to nature that draws Venus and Gaia into a very close relationship. It is also why working with flowers, herbs, crystals and all Gaia's gifts creates such a powerful magic.
Venus + intention + focus + Gaia's gifts = magnetism.
Work with her beauty, e.g. flowers, and you shall get a powerful and magnetic force of magic at your finger tips. We take herbal remedies to assist our health as Mother Earth has everything to put balance back into every situation, whether it is our health or finances. You are tapping into the powerful forces of universal,

quantum mechanics of manifestation and transformation. The nature kingdom supplies tools of beauty to assist you in empowering and magnifying your desires. The empress in the tarot is surrounded by nature's lush bounty. Why? Because she is all that. Are you ready to become your radiant version of the Empress? This gives new meaning to the term 'Be Still.' Be still and become all that which you are in truth embodied to become. "Let go, let God" is a deep and divine truth. Meditate on it: it has so many layers of teaching within it.

Working our magic, opening and healing our hearts, magnetising all things good are so important. The health of our beautiful world depends on it. As our hearts heal, as the divine feminine heals, in men as well as women, as higher levels of love energy are attained that is when the veils of our earth shall be lifted, the elemental kingdoms and nature devas shall dance back into our sight and life as we know it shall evolve into a higher dimension. So with pure intention allow yourself to experience unlimited joy and love, it has the power to heal worlds.

A Venus Recipe for Internalising your Love-full Nature

Red wine, red grape juice or pomegranate juice

1 Cinnamon stick

½ tsp of vanilla or a vanilla pod

1 tsp of Damiana: this herb energises your sexual organs

A pinch nutmeg powder

2 cardamom pods

2 tbs of rose water

Honey to taste

Simmer ingredients in a pot for 5 minutes. Allow to cool slightly, the flavours will improve if left for a bit longer, even an hour or two. Strain the liquid and pour into a nice glass. This can be shared with a loved one as a special pre-romantic night wine, with the intention of sharing some heightened love.

Make it for yourself to enhance and fortify your own loving and sensual allure. These herbs and spices are designed to feed your inner fire. As your drink the wine, see it infusing your body with beauty and magnetic light. Your hormones and endocrine system are refortified, radiating an allure, feel how sexy and beautiful you are, truly enjoy yourself and know you are love and worthy of being loved.

Hold the wine and say:

"Beautiful Venus, Radiant Aphrodite

Please bless my wine and inner light

Activate my love within me this night

I AM the goddess who shines so bright

Full of flavour and sensual delight."

Feel the energy of your intent pour into your wine, your hands cupped around the glass, universal energy flowing in and activating your ingredients and desire. As you drink your wine visualise your intent, see it infusing every cell in your body, a vision of your radiance attracting your hearts desire, inflaming your desire and vital energy infusing your manifestation magic.

Venus Perfume

This is a blend of oils to create an attraction perfume. These oils vibrate love energy, infusing your aura with love and beauty. By activating it with your intent you can magically charge it to build your confidence, attract love, create sexual allure, build sexual energy, allow your imagination to create your own personal intent and watch the magic flow around you.

Love Drawing Blend

Use essential oils of:

Jasmine - sensual and calming, confidence in self

Rose - love, commitment, sensual enhancement, abundance, heart healing

Lavender - calming, protective, transforms fear into allowing

Vanilla - warm sensual and attracting, adds confidence and strength

Oils that can be added as an extra:

Patchouli - adds power, sexual energy and strong manifestation qualities but 1 or 2 drops is enough

Sandalwood - adds a spiritual, tantric energy

Ylang Ylang - an aphrodisiac

Add your oils to a base oil like jojoba or almond oil. Once again, hold the blend and infuse it with your intention and love. Invoke the Venus chant and build up an intense energy of focus as you visualise and feel your intent. When your energy feels focused and strong, blow a small breath into the blend. This seals the blend and truly infuses your intent into the mix.

Use it as:

A personal perfume blend

To dress candles

Add to a bath

Put a little in your liquid soap or shampoo

Use it in the knot ritual with Radha

Place some in an oil diffuser

Use in a massage oil

Let your imagination run with it

Mary Magdalene

Mary comes to teach us about forgiveness, of ourselves and of anyone who may have hurt or compromised us. Mary had to learn how to love herself unconditionally; she was continually attacked by many for the role she played as close friend and lover of Jesus. Mary's presence challenged people, her light was strong and she was very close to a man who all wanted to be close to. She had an intelligence that absorbed what Jesus taught and she was able to embody his teachings. Many say she became his closest companion and lover. This alone has caused her name to create so much controversy for centuries.

I have also read through the teachings of the Hathors that Mary was an initiate of the Isis Temples. She was taught the sacred tantric practices of divine sexual union. It was planned that she would then connect with Jesus and they would fall in love so that through her sacred feminine teachings initiate his energy and through their love making infuse him with divine energy that would assist him in his ascension.

As you can imagine her love for him was deep and profound, so when it came time for him to be tortured, die and then ascend, it was a massive deep grief and loss for Mary. No matter how switched on she may have been, this was a massive challenge for her, to live the teachings of her Master and let him go. More can be read on this in Tom Kenyon's books.

Mary's challenges were many in a fairly unforgiving world. So she comes forth to assist us now to collect all the parts of ourselves that have been scattered over time and space due to the misinterpretations of Christ's teachings. Women really did come off second best and that was not his intention at all. I believe it is a grief for him that his teachings have been so distorted and punishing for women. Maybe it was the deep seated anger at Mary for sharing such a place with Jesus that began the torture and hunt on woman who embodied anything extraordinary, such as midwives and so-called witches. The beast was aroused and the lion roared and he blew his rage and need for domination at all things out of his control. The fear of losing control is great. Atlantis was lost to us due to esoteric manipulations that were driven by egos out of control and driven by their need to control. The pain of forgetfulness was aroused and it unleashed a monster bent on lashing out at all things that provoked a distant memory of his loss. This is a universal pain, a pain that causes a deep wound to be activated, a memory of our true nature as being one with god and co-creators. So now it is our time to heal and equalise the imbalance.

Mary Magdalene's Bag of Love

This pouch or small bag is about collecting the parts of you that are in need of healing; they are represented by different herbs and crystals. It is a small bag of self love and healthy intent for self. Held together in a small pouch they sing together, creating a magical talisman to support your healing and growth. I was unsure of what to do for Mary's gift but this is what I was shown. Her message is that great healing can take place in simple ways, with intention, fun and joy driving the moment all things are possible. This time is about creating love-infused rituals that can work towards building a new light body and love-infused experience. The bag is a link to your higher self, angels and the fairy realm, all of whom are ready to be of service to you. It is a two way healing; they just love to play and support us in our creative and love infused healing.

It is recommended that you re-empower your bag every full moon by refreshing the oils, leaving it out under the full moon to empower the crystal and herbs. Hold your bag regularly, infusing it with your loving intent, running your fingers through the herbs and noting how they are working for you. Thank the ingredients for their service; keep her alive by using and playing with her.

Carry the pouch with you when you need a boost of energy or some extra protection

Place under your pillow for sleep time healing

Place on your altar for amplification of its healing

Hold during your meditation time or place it on your body

Making it

Find a small bag or pouch, or make one using a colour that appeals. It could simply be some fabric that you tie into a pouch. Keep it small enough to carry in your handbag. Red, pink or green are good heart colours.

Red or pink rose petals dried: they hydrate your energy with pure love, which then attracts even more love into your life. Rose will call in the angels of love and the lost parts of your heart. She will purify and sanctify your love.

Dried Yarrow: yarrow is a fairy herb with wonderful magic around her. She heals any wounds buried in your heart and seals your light body off to any unfriendly intrusions. Yarrow is the herb of boundaries so she helps you see when to say no and who is not acting in your best interests. Yarrow will collect the parts of yourself that others have taken.

Vanilla Bean: vanilla brings potency to your intent and blend, adding a powerful and warm scent to the mix. Vanilla is musky and draws love your way.

Damiana Herb: brings healing to your sexuality, displacing the darkness and wounding, replacing it with energised life force and vitality.

Dried Apple Seeds: another very fairy ingredient, the seeds represent new growth in the area of love and relationships. The apple seeds offer support for new beginnings and ways of being in love with yourself and in creating healthy relationships. The apple is a symbol of Venus and Aphrodite.

Cinnamon Stick or Powder: cinnamon brings energy; she energises your life force and libido. When we are healing it is vital to keep revitalising ourselves, to regenerate as we let go and release the old ways. Cinnamon will feed the fires - in more ways than one!

Your Love Drawing Oil Blend: adds a lovely scent to keep the mix alive or

A couple of drops of rose oil will bring the angels of love in

Rose Geranium: for balance and protection of your sensitive emotional centre

Bergamot to bring some positive sunshine into your life, displacing depression or repression

Patchouli: to ground, empower and energise your mix.

Rose Quartz: rose quartz is a great general heart healing gem; she will draw the energies of the mix into her field of light and amplify the energy on a whole new level for you. The stones seem to take on the scent of the mix which is totally lovely.

Place all your ingredients in a bowl, run your fingers through the mix, enjoying the feel and scent of it. Place the ingredients in the bag and say:

"Roses and yarrow

Vanilla and apple

Cinnamon for heat and

Damiana oh so sweet

Angels and fairies of Mary's Light

Enchant my bag of healing this night

Weaving my heart and soul together

So that forevermore I AM as one."

All the ingredients can be found easily. Her message was to make this a soul quest; finding the herbs is part of the ritual. Each time you find one it is reclamation of that part of yourself. They can be found as teas, bags of healing herbs in health food shops and even in your local supermarket in the cooking section. Have fun with it and make it yours.

A Prayer to enlist Mary's help

One of Mary's favourite oils is rosemary. It cleanses and purifies your personal space, renewing your energy and stimulating your vital forces. Rosemary helps you remember who you are, assisting in yourself healing and regeneration.

Anoint yourself with some rosemary oil or pick some of the fresh herb to place near your meditation space. An aura spray made with rosemary and rutilated quartz is very effective. Then say:

"I call upon Mary Magdalene to please assist me with the deep healing of my heart. Please help me to forgive myself and all others that we may be free to be true again. I offer my heart to the light for healing, so that I may regenerate and radiate my true soul essence again. I ask that all others who have played a part in my story also receive this healing if they are willing. I ask for this healing on all levels of my being and in all space and time, past, present and future. Infuse my being with pure love that it may radiate through out all the cells of my body, light body and chakra system bringing me into a state of radiant wholeness. Thank you. Om Mani Padme Hum."

Radha and Krishna: A Divine Union

Radha is the goddess of romantics and lovers. She was the beloved mistress of Krishna. The story says that Radha had an unearthly beauty; she caught the attention of a young Krishna and began a deep and intense relationship, filled with love, passion and challenge. Radha comes along to help desperate romantics fulfil their desires no matter how hard the challenge. The challenge of their relationship was that she was never able to have Krishna all to herself; he was an embodiment of love, a love that was to be shared on a global level, spiritually as well as at times physically. Radha's challenge was to find balance with her intense love and passion for Krishna with an understanding that her love would never possess him. He loved her and their union was ecstatic but he knew his role and fulfilled it well.

The message here is that to love ecstatically is a blessing but do not become too attached as often it is the divine dancing, but as humans we want to hold on to every ecstatic moment. Maybe it is ok to love in the moment and feel safe and have enough self love to keep flowing with life and not hang on. True love can only be fulfilled when we set it free, then it remains pure. This does not mean that all love will pass through our fingers and slip away but don't limit your ideas of what love can be. Radha is a pure being, living in a state of Samadhi, but she is also human and desires the experience of divine union with another compatible soul. They symbolise the union of love, of oneness and divine union.

Call on Radha for:

Blessings on romance

Passion and romantic love

Support during a break up

Experiencing your own sensuality

Falling in love with the divine

Experiencing love through nature or devotional chanting

Knot of Love Ritual

This is a ritual to create a bracelet to draw a pure source of love and passion into your life.

Start this on a Friday night, the day of Venus.

Find some pink, green and/or white thread (colours of heart and love)

Tie 6 knots along the length of thread (6 is a number of love and the number of points on the Star of David, symbol of heart chakra)

As you tie each knot chant:

"Om Radha Krishnaya Namaha"

(Om and salutations to that single being of love, manifesting as the lovers Radha and Krishna)

Then place some of your love oil blend or favourite oil on the knotted thread.

Repeat the chant every day, running your fingers over the knots. Tie on your ankle, wrist or leave on your altar or hanging from your car mirror.

Summary of Light Codes 6 and 7

This layer is the portal to the sacred part of you that split off when you began incarnating. It assists with your communication with the divine; through meditation and prayer we can heal this breach. By embodying these Light Codes we are integrating self love and compassion into our DNA, thus creating an elimination of the heavier dross of guilt, hate and envy. As this occurs we become more receptive to the love and the light of our higher selves. We then magnetise the flow of divine knowing more fully into our lives. This is the Holy Spirit of ourselves and our true I AM presence. Working with this layer is very important, to validate and fulfil our right as a spiritual being having a human experience and that it is ok to enjoy all that it has to offer. Release all guilt and totally enjoy every moment.

Thymus Chakra

The thymus chakra is an extra one, found above the heart on the sternum. It has only recently been recognised as a chakra on its own. This chakra is being developed to assist us with the shift into the fifth dimension. It is a step up into the throat chakra. Through higher loving thoughts and words we can bridge the space between us and our guides, masters and angels. She is a lovely turquoise/aquamarine colour. See emerald green flowing up from the heart and blue flowing down from the throat to create this sublime aqua shade over your thymus. This will improve your immunity and open you up to your inner spiritual gifts that became closed and forgotten after the fall of Atlantis. Amazing healing powers are stored in this chakra; she takes the waves of Light coming through your crown chakra and converts them into a radiance that supports you to stay attuned to your higher self. As this happens, you become a beacon of healing and transpersonal support for yourself on a personal level as well as a universal level. Your own health will improve as your immunity grows stronger; this chakra collects all the lost parts of yourself, heals them and reintegrates your wholeness. As you heal, reintegrate and return to wholeness this then turns you into a powerful spiritual healer that can truly make a difference. I call this the Holy Grail, as we find ourselves we shall become the mythical Holy Grail that man has searched for.

Crystals for Thymus Health

Apophyllite (green), aquamarine, celestite, turquoise (not for essence making)

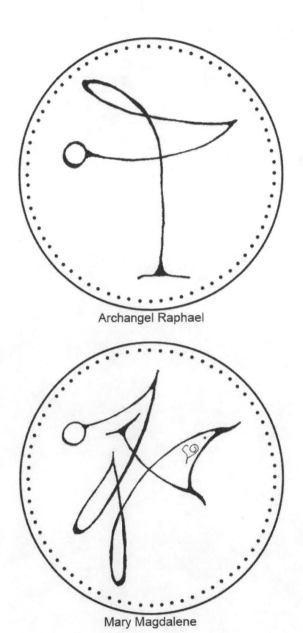

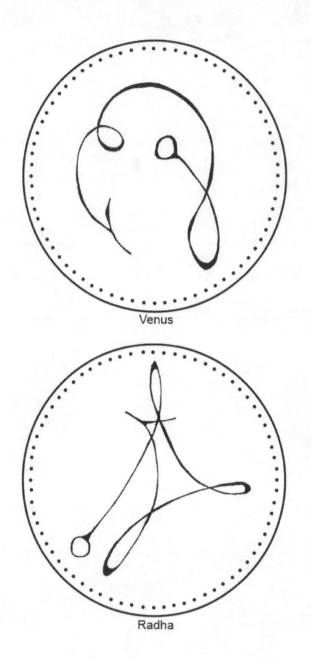

Krishna

Chapter 6

Throat Chakra

8th and 9th Light Codes

Archangel Gabriel

Associated body parts: throat, thyroid, parathyroid, neck, shoulders, hearing problems.

The throat chakra is a doorway into the higher dimensions, it resonates at 5th dimensional energy and ushers us into that timeless place of spiritual liberation. It is from our throat chakra that we learn to speak, this is the communication capital of your personal domain, to verbalise our needs, our opinions, our ideas and thus our creative expression. Creativity is our link to the creator and becoming a co-creator, so it is all very grand and exciting. When the throat chakra is blocked it reveals a separation from one's divine expression. Think of how many have lost their lives over the eons because they dared to express their spiritual essence. The count of lost lives during the Inquisition alone is well into the 100,000's. The favourite reason to behead, burn, hang, drown and torture these poor souls was because they were branded a witch. What was a witch? Someone who helped the poor with their knowledge of healing and midwifery, or maybe someone who spoke up for others less fortunate or maybe she was just so radiant with light that it annoyed the big in control fearful ones. Whatever the cause, it left a pretty harsh scar on the many who met their ends this way. Do you hate anything up around your neck? If so you are probably one who met this end in another life time.

It is from our throat chakra that we use words to shape our lives. I love the term "wordsmith", someone who chooses his words so carefully; he crafts his life with language for he has learned the true power of the spoken word. As we ascend into higher vibrational fields of life and potential it is imperative that we learn to express ourselves wisely, for eventually even all thoughts will have a response and reaction in one's life. It is quite an initiation to learn this mastery, for we have become basically quite lazy in our thoughts and words. Sometimes we just babble away, getting lost in the woes of life and in what Mrs X down the road just did to poor little Miss M. Really none of that is any of our business, in fact what anyone else thinks or does is none of our business, whether they like us or not, none of it matters. Sure if someone is compromising your boundaries, then yes speak up, be honest and clear then move on. Don't waste your precious breath on things that don't matter as you become drained and end up carrying a lot of negative energy around with you.

This chakra is where we develop clairaudient skills; we can channel spiritual truths from masters and guides. This is why it is so important to care for this centre as you seriously do not want to attract lower life forms and start channelling their darkness. Most of us on a path of truth are protected from this until we have developed our higher states of being. When someone has not purified enough of their field of light they are more vulnerable to attracting mischievous spirits looking to have a bit of fun. Cleansing our field of light is so important in order not to pick up errant floating negative energy; it can happen at no fault of yours. If you are radiating light and still processing and evolving then you are a little more vulnerable to lost souls hoping on for a ride as they see your light and are attracted to it, like a moth drawn into the light. Just remember to do a clearing and cord cutting with AA Michael each day to clear and upgrade your system and light body.

As we learn to balance this chakra key of non-attachment and balance we ascend into a higher vibration. Spirit is more able to connect with you and your creative expression becomes more alive. This chakra colour is blue; I see it as a blue cape, placed around our shoulders signifying our ascent into our wisdom and clear expression of it. As I said earlier there is quite a strong initiation at this point, by learning to be still and letting life flow around you, learning to master your reactions to various situations that arise just to push your buttons and seeing all life as a part of yourself, something to be embraced and accepted, you will move through this easily. Well it does take practice and vigilance, use your blue cape to see through the illusions of things, your wisdom and intuition will grow stronger and clearer and mastery shall follow.

Sound is an immensely powerful energy. It is said that by using pure, high frequency sound that the Egyptians were able to move the mammoth blocks of stone that built the pyramids. They had help from beings that travelled here from another planet; they taught the humans how to use the magic of sound to reverse gravity so that the blocks became weightless. That is the power of sound. What about music you love, it can totally lift your mood; this then lifts your vibration and deeply charges your cells and beingness with healing and positive energy. Sacred chants can carry one into the deeply spiritual state of Samadhi and heavy metal can potentially cause much heavier states of expression. There are sound frequencies that can alter our mind and lift our vibration. These sounds mimic the frequencies of monks who have spent lifetimes in meditation in order to ascend. The frequencies are alpha, beta, theta and delta. There are others but these are the main four. The first two assist with concentration and creative expression, the last two, theta and delta take the brain into deep states of meditation, assisting visualisation and brain chemical balance. The more we practice these states of mind the easier it becomes to access them and start becoming them. In doing this it is so much easier to access our own intuition and psychic awareness. The right sounds and music can greatly assist in elevating your consciousness into higher states of awareness.

Another form of communication to consider is the communication of your inner body. How do your bodily functions communicate? Your cells, glands, organs, blood, digestion are all dependant on how well your system communicates. So what is it that drives that communication system? Your genetics, how you feel about life and yourself, do you love and honour yourself? How you interact with life has a huge bearing on how well your body assimilates life. It comes back again to how we communicate and create ourselves and our life. If you love yourself, love life and honour your needs the chances are you will be a healthier human being. Get to know who you are, what you like and don't like, how to say no and how to say yes to all things that nourish your life and learn the difference between the two. This sacred chakra has a huge bearing on your metabolism. Think about the thyroid gland, it is one of the major players in your metabolism, care for this vital part of yourself as she can teach you a lot about yourself and what works for you. There are so many levels to this chakra and how we communicate with life.

So as you can see the power of sound is indeed a potent one and one that we must master, first through our speech and wise use of our words. Unblock that fear that ties up your throat from speaking your truth, no one will behead you this time around and if they don't like what you say then so be it, not your problem. So long as you know that you have acted in integrity and love that is all that matters. For as you express so to do you create, quite a responsibility, especially as we start ascending into higher octaves of life and every thought can become a reality. This is why spirit will test you on this one until you get it together; this is for your own protection as much as anything else. As you get to know yourself better and what it is that you are feeling it shall become easier and easier to know what to say in any given moment, your boundaries will be healthy and yourself love button will be turned on. Self love is so important as it sets up an inner radar that can inform you if a certain experience is not resonating for your highest good. So set that love button on and allow it to be your radar.

Light Codes 8 and 9

These codes epitomise that we are "I AM Divine Voice". Through the cosmic sounds we express we create rainbow prisms of light and diamonds of joy. This is another divinely Lemurian centre for it is with these Light Codes that we truly begin to epitomise our divinity in our human form. Through these codes we enter into a true relationship with our divine selves, our soul and Great Spirit. We co-create and live in tune with the divine directives that our higher centres channel down to us. We sort out the transmissions of light that we are receiving and turn them into useable and workable expressions of life on the earth plane. These Light Codes are like a translator service of cosmic information into understandable and reachable language that we then turn into physical manifestations of joyous life expression. Joy is a key word here; joy lifts the vibration and puts you in touch with these frequencies in an easily accessible way.

Archangel Gabriel

AA Gabriel is the supernal messenger of god. He is like the breath of god, entering our bodies and lightening them with divine life and light. This breath caresses our whole system, opening us to a higher vision of ourselves and life. We then learn to verbalise our truth as it becomes clear in the light of our sacred breath. Our sacred breath is what carries our sacred sounds and truth into the world around us, carrying as such the message of god, for we are all the embodiment of this holy force.

It is said that it was AA Gabriel who informed Mary and Elizabeth of the impending birth of their divine sons, Jesus and John the Baptist, once again being the holy messenger. Gabriel supports a child as it prepares to incarnate, assisting them in the womb, whispering to them of their journey they are about to begin. Gabriel is often called on by women wanting to conceive as he is known for his midwifery skills. Gabriel is airy and yet watery at the same time, he offers emotional healing and a gift of communication and an implementation of one's skills. He shines his light on all our creative and spiritual doings, assisting us to actualise that which he whispered to us whilst still in the womb. His watery nature drenches us in a sublime hydration of light, like watering a dehydrated plant and watching its magnificence unfold.

AA Gabriel can guide us into the deepest depths of our being, assisting us to heal and cleanse what is blocking our way forward.

His breath and watery presence act as magic transformers, turning lead into gold. As we learn to communicate wisely and with compassion we shall truly reconnect with our Atlantean gifts and reconnect the hole that was left by its destruction. All these angels have a part to play in reconstructing a new and enlightened way of being, of healing the damage done and exposing where the wounding lies, thus erasing it from our DNA so that we can step forward again as enlightened beings. This angel also known as Strength of God assists all creative people to communicate their creative gifts to the world, whether it is writing, art, music…it does not matter, they are all divine tools of creative expression.

Throat Chakra Crystals

These crystals can cross over with the thymus and third eye crystals at times. In doing this they support the link between one chakra's working and the next.

Turquoise, beautiful cerulean blue turquoise links heaven on earth through its sky blue colour and rich mineral state, she brings happiness and heightened awareness to this centre. This stone is also quite protective, blocking lower astral life forms from attaching to this communication centre. You certainly do not want to channel dark thoughts and words. She will assist you to receive clear guidance, to hear from your heart and speak from a place of deep truth. The copper in the stone will also align you with Venus energy….love!

Aquamarine is very cooling and cleansing. She will hydrate your system and improve your metabolism. Because of her watery nature she will assist you to express your emotions comfortably and bring to the surface any hidden emotional blocks. This stone then helps to keep them in balance and restore harmony. Aquamarine heals and resurrects the divine feminine, assisting in psychic opening and increased intuition.

Angelite is another lovely soft blue stone. As the name implies she connects your communication centre to the angels. Their messages may appear in songs, on billboards, in a book or other unexpected places but with this stone's help you will be awakened to their significance and alert to seeing them. She will harmonise your throat to a higher state allowing much freedom to occur.

Chrysocolla is a goddess stone. She assists with the integration of your internal goddess energy. She will help you speak from a place of gentle sovereignty, assisting you to hold your space and be in truth with yourself. This crystal also cleanses your energy pathways and realigns them with your healthy best, especially good for therapists after a long day of clients.

Kyanite is an amazing mineral. She cuts through what no longer serves one's highest good and by revivifying one's system allows the new to enter. She is a silvery blue which elevates her vibration assisting one to connect more clearly to one's guides. I also find her rather protective as she puts up a shield of light to bounce away what does not resonate with love. Kyanite also revivifies the system helping to prevent burnout.

Apatite is a beautiful peacock blue. This stone assists teachers and other public speakers to get past their anxiety and speak clearly; she seems to clear the fog and open the throat. Another very valuable gift of this stone is its ability to balance the metabolism. A crystal essence made with this stone is great for people wishing to lose weight. She helps with tissue regeneration and repair. Apatite also stimulates the psychic senses assisting us to see clearly and deepen meditation.

Aqua Aura is clear quartz bonded with gold and she is a very beautiful stone. Her lovely aqua colour will raise your vibration and connect you with angels and guides. She is a feel-good stone, lifting the mood and enhancing all psychic abilities. Carrying a piece around with you will boost your aura's energy giving you a little more light to carry you through.

Larimar, beautiful larimar just has to be included in the throat chakra section. She is the colour of a soft, tranquil ocean. Her influence is one of bringing calm to troubled times, a memory of Atlantis and dolphins, goddesses and ancient temples. Wear this magical stone to uplift and yet calm your spirit; her memories will trigger your own and magic will flow again. Larimar is great for the nervous system, for cooling the body and empowering sensitive individuals.

You will notice many of these stones boost your energy or clear it. Remember the throat chakra carries a lot of influence over your metabolism so use them to maintain your health and well being. Better to maintain than try to it fix later.

Flower Essence – Throat Chakra

Native Rosemary

Native rosemary is a strong plant; she is able to with stand harsh conditions and still thrive. We need this strength at times to stand in our truth, when even loved ones may not be handling the changes you are making. Remember your vital energy can be drained by not being true to yourself, of allowing others to dominate your mind. There is vulnerability at the throat centre, wanting to keep the peace and all those other power play offs. It is also a centre where those who are open can have uninvited spirit attachments occur that can cause quite a distortion in how one relates to life. Always be aware of your thoughts and if they seem somehow out of alignment with your normal self then check in and do AA Michaels prayer of protection. This should clear and move on the disruption. This is a chakra worthy of good maintenance and care.

Very protective essence, negativity will just bounce off enabling you to hear your own voice over the controlling needs of others.

Assists you to express your own truth

Good for sinus, ear, throat and thyroid problems

Protects children from harsh environments, assisting them to stay here, grounded and able to feel their own boundaries and angelic guides.

Protects one from the reaction others have to you speaking your truth, gives you the will to stay true to self

Works well with AA Michael, dolphin and whale healing

Brings you into alignment with your higher self, strengthening your clairaudience and protecting you against negative entity attachments and manipulations.

As the throat chakra heals and rises in vibration the colour goes from light blue to dark blue, violet blue, silver blue and gold/royal blue.

Essential Oils for Throat Chakra

The throat is quite a speed station for incoming and outgoing data: it is processing very quickly and often acting on automatic. Because of this a lot of different types of energy can be processed through here. There are times when we have to deal with all types of people in varying stages of evolvement. It is not that we compromise who we are to engage with them but it can be challenging to communicate on certain levels. Take going through divorce for instance – it is not always going to be pleasant chatty communication. So the oils are about keeping this energy vortex clear and purified, this allows the throat to stay in a space of purity so we can connect with our higher self and guides. When it gets clogged and grimy we run the risk of negative attachments. Negative energy hates purifying oils as the scent repels them. A great tip is to keep some white Tiger Balm or similar product in your bag. If the atmosphere is feeling a bit heavy put a little balm on the back of your neck as it keeps it clear and protected. Great for crowded shopping centres.

Eucalyptus clears the ears, nose and throat passageways, going even deeper into the lungs clearing our breath. She opens our throat chakra for better communications and to focus intent. Any vibes left from negative words are effectively cleared, whether it was you or another speaking inappropriately. Often if a conversation leaves you feeling drained or just not quite right then you need to clear it as you do not need negative energy imprinting you when you are healing yourself confidence. Use the oil in an oil burner during a cleansing ritual or in a room mister.

Tea Tree works in a similar way to eucalyptus, deeply cleansing and clearing any negative vibes we may have picked up in our daily doings. Both these oils are great for your immune system, which shows us how important it is to our health to keep our energy bodies clear and light. Tea tree clears any fungal issues and used in dilution will help keep your gums nice and healthy.

Lemongrass is an antidepressant and lifts exhaustion. Both these conditions can be due to low metabolism and thyroid imbalance. She lifts one's spirit and gets things moving again. Never use undiluted on skin as it will burn. It is antiseptic and prevents the spread of disease. A drop on the hand of a body worker provides a wonderful screen of light that protects from any negative transference during the healing session. This protection works physically as well as spiritually.

Chamomile is a wonderful calmative as sometimes the thyroid can be over active causing hyper active behaviour. Or maybe one has a confronting conversation coming up and nervous tension is building. Use a little roman chamomile to calm yourself so that ideas and conversation flow with ease. The oil will effectively calm your nervous system making room for clear-headed decisions and speech.

Lemon is so cleansing and uplifting that it had to be included. Lemon will cleanse, uplift and clear mental blocks, allowing clarity to return. She invigorates the immune system which can take quite a thrashing when we are confused and doubting ourselves, common when having to speak up for ourselves. Allow lemon to blow away the cobwebs and illuminate your truth.

Ritual of Activation for Throat Chakra and Light Codes 8 and 9

A blue candle

Sage or suitable oil spritzer to cleanse space

Chosen essential oil for candle and throat chakra

Throat sigil…AA Gabriel

Chosen crystal

Throat chakra essence to take or bless chakra with

Cleanse room with sage or spritzer

Place candle in a safe container. Sigil maybe carved into wax or placed safely beneath candle

Anoint the candle with chosen oil and light

Take a couple of drops of the essence and place a drop on your throat chakra

Say prayer of protection

Put yourself into a relaxed state, do some deep breathing, calming your thoughts and mind, feeling all your muscles releasing and letting go, be very present and willing to give yourself this time to heal.

Invoke AA Gabriel

"In the name of love and light I ask my guides, celestial helpers and Archangel Gabriel to please open, activate and balance my

throat chakra, placing within it the crystalline structures and sacred geometry I need to fully bring my throat chakra into its highest vibration and health activation. I ask that the corresponding Light Codes 8 and 9 and DNA be brought into perfect harmony with my soul's highest expression now. I command the activation of the 8th and 9th Light Codes now, bringing them into their highest level of presence. I ask for this healing in all time and space, past, present and future, clearing all past illusion and bringing me fully into the present moment. I am so grateful for this healing, thank you, Om Mani Padme Hum."

Sit or lie quietly allowing the guides and angels to do their healing work with you. Breathe into your throat, see a wash of different shades of blue, all swirling around your throat, ears and mouth. The blues feel very calming and uplifting, the energy of the angels moves through the blue bringing a sense of upliftment, joy and peace. Your throat feels quite relaxed and open, allowing for any messages to clearly reach you. Stay with this as long as you need to, enjoying the soft, floating sensation. The blue now saturates every cell in your body, truly activating this precious Light Code.

Stay with this as long as you wish.

The seed sound for this chakra is Ham (Huum)

Chanting this sound will assist with the healing and activation of this chakra.

Animal Totem

An animal totem for this chakra is the whale. No one can deny the sounds whales make are just awesome. Their frequencies travel for miles under the water. It is said that these sounds are balancing and equalising the harmonics and lay lines of the earth. That the whales and dolphins are originally from Sirius and have come here to use the creative magic of sound to help us re evolve mother earth, to hold her steady and rebirth her. The sounds they make are totally telepathic and sonic, truly highly evolved beings. They bring such joy when they are seen breaching from the water, a memory of times long forgotten.

Aboriginals when found in their true environments are also said to be amazing telepaths. I have heard stories of them that are quite amazing; they live from their spirit, allowing it to guide them in their lives and survival. They have been known to telepathically communicate to their friends hundreds of miles away, letting them know they are on their way. There is so much to learn, one thing I have realised that the more innocence we allow to redevelop within us the more our true gifts shall return. Imagine if we were telepathic now and everyone could read everyone else's mind … mmm, a bit chaotic I suspect.

Goddess Work

Saraswati

Hymn to Saraswati

"May Saraswati-goddess of knowledge, who is praised by the wise, who is the wife of the creator-reside on my tongue."

Saraswati's symbol is a swan; the swan is able to distinguish between substance and illusion, truth and falsehood. She also is often seen sitting on a lotus and carrying prayer beads.

Saraswati is a goddess of the spoken word; her name means "the flowing one". As the flowing one she flows the creative impulse, creating existence, assisting with this vital task where and when she is needed. She is an Indian goddess of high degree. It is said she created the Gayatri Mantra, one of the most famous and sacred mantras, known as the essence of all mantras. The Gayatri Mantra is able to bring activation into the seven luminous bodies of our light body. Each of the individual syllables of this mantra contains a seed sound that resonates with the seven planes of light. As we regularly practise this mantra we build strength and vitality the divine energy within us that connects us to our divinity. The OM mantra is the beginning sound, in the beginning there was nothing, Brahma (Indian God) was lost as to how to create order out of a sea of nothingness, the goddess spoke from within him, and she said "Through knowledge, from knowledge will come creative action". As Brahma felt this truth blossom within him he opened his mouth and the sacred OM came forth and began the process of creative order in the universe. In Saraswati's realm speech comes from the place of truth within you, words are an expression of cosmic clarity, realities and truth, never superficial and meaningless.

This highly intelligent and beautiful goddess will inspire us in all that we do on a creative level. The throat chakra is a very creative centre because as we speak and think so to do we create our world. She will assist anyone, from students struggling with school work, to teachers, artists, writers, musicians and creators of sacred texts so that the understanding and integration of the divine continues to expand and grow.

Expression of our creative selves is our true purpose, not to get lost in competitive programs of achievement and survival but the gracious use and expression of our creative gifts and self expression. If you are stuck and lost with this then Saraswati is your go-to girl for some inspired assistance, she is the ultimate muse. Her assistance can also be called upon to help you when a situation arises that requires careful and sensitive communication with another, maybe like a job interview or confronting situation.

Ritual for Creative Assistance

Create a lovely altar:

If you have an image of Saraswati, include it. (internet is a great source of pictures)

Place some flowers and an orange on your altar

Sandalwood incense or lotus if you can find it

Mala beads

Some special blue items

A bowl with a blue candle, some ground coconut and rice

Saraswati's sigil either on candle or nearby

Chosen oil and crystals mixed in with rice and coconut

Choose a night after the new moon, so that a crescent moon is visible, leave the altar set up until the full moon to keep building the energy.

Place your candle in a fire proof bowl with the rice, coconut, oils and crystals

Write on a piece of paper what creative challenge you are requiring assistance with; place this under the fire proof bowl

Say:

"I AM the centre of the divine universe,

I AM the sacred mandala of existence

Graceful Saraswati your assistance I reverently request."

Light your candle and incense, allow the scent to cleanse and uplift your space, sit and relax with the energy. Using your breath, draw in Saraswati's energy with your in breath and visualise your request as answered with your out breath. Feel the peace of effortless achievement and success, feel gratitude and grace filling your energy.

Chant Saraswati's mantra: *"OM Aim Saraswatyai Namaha"*

(Ohm aim suh-ruh-swah-tyai nuh-muh-huh)

"I bow to the goddess of speech."

If you have mala beads and feel drawn to, chant the mantra 108 times to energise your request. The beads then also carry and hold the energy for you. Wear them to keep your light body energised.

Sit in your sacred place enjoying the energy. Do not stress and strain to find any answers, just let go and trust the universe to support you in your quest.

When you are finished put the candle out and leave your altar set up. Each night until the full moon repeat the ritual (no need to do more written requests, just leave it under your candle). When the night of the full moon is over, either bury your request in the garden or burn it in your candle.

Eat your orange, enjoy every juicy mouthful, see the bright orange colour firing up your corresponding creative centre, know that the orange has taken on the energy of Saraswati and that your creative knowing is charged and ready to go. By eating the orange you are activating your inner Saraswati.

Then sit back and await your inspiration or shift in flow to occur.

Mantras to Empower

Use to empower your ability to manifest:

"OM Aim Hrim Saraswati Namaha."

(Ohm ai-eem hreem suh-rah-swah-tyai nuh-muh-huh)

"Om, I bow to the flowing one whose essence is wisdom and the power to manifest."

Gayatri Mantra

Use to achieve a natural enlightened state

"Om Bhur Om Bhuvaha Om Swaha

Om Maha Om Janaha Om Tapaha Om Satyam

Om Tat Savitur Varenyam

Bhargo Devasya Dhimahi

Dhiyo Yonaha Prachodayat."

(Om Boor Om Boo-vah-hah Om Swah-ha

Om Mah-ha Om Jah-nah-ha Om Saht-yahm

Om Taht Sah-vee-toor Vah-rein-yum

Bhahr-goh Dei-vahs-yah Dhee-mah-hee

Dhee-yoh Yoh-nah-hah Prah-choh-dah-yaht)

"Oh self-effulgent light that has given birth

To all the lokas (spheres of consciousness)

Who is worthy of worship and appears

Through the orbit of the sun, illuminate our

Intellect"

All the mantras in this book are basically attributable to Saraswati as it is her energy that gives us the spoken word to create with, whatever that creation is. Be it health, wealth, creativity it is all the same.

Maat

Maat is an ancient Egyptian goddess of fairness. She weighs one's life against the weight of a feather to see how balanced a life you lived when it is time to pass over. Maat is in charge of sacred harmony, linking the mundane world with the divine. Her work includes fairness, justice, truth and keeping a state of grace alive. In Egypt sacred rituals existed to preserve the state of Maat. She is very connected to the ancient Egyptian god Thoth and together they work to educate and maintain divine balance and grace.

This simple ritual can be used to request guidance about situations that you are unsure of. Confusion is common as we ascend our spiral back to wholeness. Situations can arise both within and in our outer world that can feel uncertain and often times maybe a little unfair. The ascending heart wishes to maintain a pure state but whilst 3D situations can still arise, we often need a little help in sorting out truth from illusion. As the throat chakra can hold a lot of self judgement, like not being able to speak up due to self doubt, Maat seems like a great support goddess to have here.

Ritual of Truth

One blue candle

Some lemon and eucalyptus oil for candle and to burn in an oil diffuser

A feather (symbol of Maat)

Maat's sigil either engraved on candle or sitting on altar with feather and candle

Say:

"From the heart of Maat

And with the Light of wisdom

Please illuminate my truth

And my pathway of peace."

Sit in a softly meditative state, an image of Maat before you, very beautiful and regal. From your heart show her your situation, let her feel your truth and sincerity about finding a fair solution. See Maat pick up her beautiful feather and wave it over you, it creates a breeze that stirs the energy around you, blending with the wonderfully purifying oils you have burning. As this goes on you can feel your burden dissolving and dissipating away. Maat looks deeply into your eyes and you experience a transmission of love and a knowing that all is going to sort itself out, that you will know exactly how to handle your current challenge. In fact it may have been removed altogether or you may have a dream that guides your actions. However the events unfold, all will be done under the loving grace of Maat. This is her gift, to uphold fairness and peace. Thank Maat and when you are ready, return to your normal state, feeling lighter and supported in your journey back to wholeness.

Summary of Light Codes 8 and 9

As we climb up the spiral in these Light Codes we are truly entering into our relationship with the divine. Remember we are one with the divine and as we turn these codes back on, we reawaken this knowing and connection. As this occurs here we can start to access the Akashic records of our soul's journey and regain the gifts and lessons of our spiritual journey. At the throat centre we have to release judgement in order to live in truth, it is here we open the doors to our own truth, because in releasing judgment we are safe to finally face our truth and embrace all that we are. As we do this we are able to, if necessary as healers, access other people's stories as well to assist with the defragmentation of old belief systems.

We also activate a healing code that is buried deeply in our DNA. This code knows how to heal us, to correct imbalances and begin our journey as enlightened beings. This code seems to be triggered when we have passed enough initiations and our essence automatically switches back on that which was programmed into us eons ago. The density of our existence for so long automatically shut these codes down until we were responsible enough to have them back. Because of the magnitude of these codes our integrity needs to be pure and in alignment with your higher self. This is why the throat area is where we finally must release all judgements, of self or others, if we are truly going to make this leap in consciousness and evolvement. Remember that clairaudience comes through the throat centre - imagine the chaos of unevolved thoughts all flying around and we can read them.

It is within this Light Code that the Violet Flame of St Germain starts to have a real influence; it burns away that which no longer serves our immortal soul, more on this in the next chapter.

Bring the unconditional love from the heart centre up into the throat, dissolving all fear and self judgment. Love yourself enough to be compassionately honest.

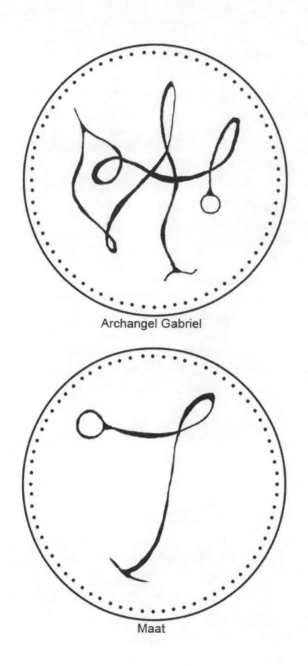

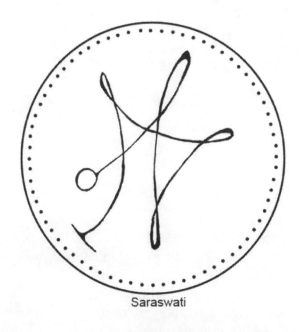
Saraswati

Chapter 7

Third-Eye Chakra

Light Code 10

Archangel Raziel

Associated body parts: pituitary gland, pineal gland, eyes, ears, brain and neurological functions.

The Third Eye is found on the forehead between the eyes. There are minor Third Eye chakras that are situated up the central line of the forehead also. The Sanskrit symbol of this chakra has only two petals, where as all the others have from four through to thousands. The two petals symbolise the freedom of the soul to fly, they are our wings. As we learn to drop judgment and see life in a somewhat objective way, we bring our two eyes into one. There is an alchemical merging within your system that marries the polarity of your being and you enter into a state of oneness. This chakra is about learning to see all life as one. Our outer life and inner life are one and the same, a reflection of who we are and how we operate. All beings are made in the image of the creator no matter their origin and all people who cross our path are as one with us, teaching, showing us and illustrating our truth. As we embrace this truth our Third Eye will grow stronger and we will see beyond the physical world, bringing us insight and an understanding of the truth hidden behind the everyday occurrences in our lives. This chakra transcends time, allowing us to come into the present moment, realising that all time is happening simultaneously, past, present and future, all possibilities that can be created and shifted from right here, right now. It is possible to do exercises to strengthen this chakra which do help but in the end you cannot forcibly open this chakra: to do so would put you at risk of damaging yourself. Many who have experimented with drugs have blown this chakra open and done some serious damage to their brain chemistry, to the point of hospitalisation in a mental illness ward. True awakening happens as we learn to spiritually embody truth and wisdom. As we become balanced in the laws of enlightenment, then our chakra petals organically open and flower unto the heavenly aspects of your spirit. Once you have embodied these truths your spiritual gifts will truly become physically manifest.

Clairvoyance is the main gift of this chakra, a gift many seek as it is great to see what is going on. To be able to see into other realities, see guides and angels, past lives and future possibilities. It is very glamorous and exciting and often has a certain spiritual arrogance that can come with it. The trap with this is that clairvoyance can open before one has truly embraced their spiritual essence. The aura has many levels as does our reality; our vibration will direct the level we work from. This then leads the person to believe they are "there", the glamour of it all covers and distracts them from continuing to embrace their spiritual evolvement and keep growing. It's like they get off at a train station and never get back on and miss most of the great journey that lies ahead of them. One's spiritual journey never stops, there is always so much more to experience and expand into. Another point about unevolved clairvoyance is that just because they "see" something does not mean it is true. A lower energy reader may attract lower energy visions, fed by unevolved spirits on the other side. It pays to be very careful who you invite into your personal space, check in and feel if the reader is a match to your spiritual light, if not it is best to not go there. A true mystic does not use clairvoyance; they just "know" what's going on, a clear and true visioning as a oneness with all life. This does not mean clairvoyance is not great. Just realise it needs to treated with respect, nurtured and used to assist one to evolve. Intuition is a higher vibrational gift than clairvoyance.

Something else to be aware of when looking into the future is that what you or someone else sees is probably not set in stone but a possible outcome based on where you are now with yourself. The blessing with this understanding is that you have the power to shift your future outcome if you are not happy with it. Never take what someone says to you as the be all and end all of your future - by doing that you have just given your power away. Listen and feel within yourself if that resonates with you as your truth. If not delete it from your mind or do a ritual to change the outcome. We will look at a ritual for this in the Goddess Section. Remember, the third-eye is your visioning tool. What you intend and focus on and giving it light through your magic eye can become so!! You are your own creator.

Through holding an image in our third-eye we have the ability to make it so. A common term for this is creative visualisation. Using our imagination we can create the picture in our mind's eye of how we would like to see our life, the third-eye then shines her light through this image and fills it with life force and projects the image out into the creative fields of potential reality to hopefully actualise your intent. The more belief one has in oneself, the more intense and clear the message will be and thus the more potential you have to succeed in your creation. True success also depends on having cleared any self sabotage programs you maybe carrying that will unconsciously kick in and undermine the power of your intent.

This is why using ritual can be so helpful when starting to reclaim your creative right to manifest your desires. The power of ritual will assist in clearing the unconscious saboteur programs and empower your intent, giving you tools to assist in the process at hand. Everything has a frequency, all thoughts, conscious and unconscious; we are continually creating our reality. Now it is time to consciously create our reality, by keeping our thoughts clear and attuned to our highest creative hopes, whether it is your health, love life, bank balance. It is time to command your life the way you want it to manifest. Using the tools provided you will find ways to keep your creative eye clear so a pure focus and intent can be attuned. Keep your thoughts attuned to a high frequency of thought and watch your life begin to manifest in an uplifting and positive way. This is so important to this Light Code, you are stepping up into true co-creative spaces and unless you work on keeping this eye clear you will not fully be initiated into higher creative work. Your personal life will reflect where you are not focusing on higher outcomes: use your personal life to fine tune your focus and goals. By keeping the mind attuned in this way you effectively begin to block negatives from entering your personal space, one's self love ratio goes up and the light body expands.

Formula for creating positive outcomes:

Intent (will, solar plexus) + focus (third-eye) + feeling (emotion, heart chakra) = manifestation

One of the best ways to help this chakra is to keep your vibration and energy clear and high. Look at ways to lift your moods, keep clear of people who zap or drain you and try to see the positive side of situations. This will ensure your "eye" stays clear and that your "seeing" is true and your "visioning" protected from negative vibes that might pollute its clarity and positive manifestation.

Light Code 10

The pineal gland contains our original etheric blueprint. It contains the light codes of our original perfection. The pineal gland allows our deepest memories to flow into our consciousness. This gland is affected by light and sounds of a pure and high frequency such as theta, gamma and delta brain waves and silence. These sounds and light build up and strengthen the pineal and our surrounding light body, protecting us from harmful electromagnetic energies and denser vibrations. The sound frequencies and light waves actually assist with the activating of our DNA light codes. Our cells expand and relax, opening to these high frequencies which match the frequencies of our evolved DNA, thus bringing them back to life. The theta and gamma frequencies bypass the density of the 3D environment that keeps us in locked and lowered awareness and breaks the barrier to an ability to activate the Light Codes and awaken. They are such a gift to us, a doorway to opportunity and awakening. The pineal is situated in the centre of our brain. As it becomes activated, it in turn switches on our Golden Crown Diamond, which is the crown that links all the higher chakras found around the head, beginning our connection back into higher states of consciousness and connection. The awakening pineal connects with our most primal cells thus carrying the awakening into our deepest physical beingness. This is the first of the divine god layers. It is no more important than the rest, in fact it would be fairly inert without the other layers, no way to actualise itself. By man saying he is ready to activate his awareness of his god self he activates this layer to connect and unfold his god self on earth.

Archangel Raziel

AA Raziel is the keeper of the mysteries, the hall of divine wonder and the sacred portal keeper of all time. These are the records of God;s eternal truth and wisdom. AA Raziel keeps the supreme wisdom of the soul safe and guides mankind to find his own wisdom and access to the hall of mysteries. The divine wisdom is held in his ray of violet light. The violet ray is the ray of magic and ritual. Through these portals of magic we learn to unravel the illusions blinding us and create an access to the divine to illuminate our truth, to create our destiny, to dissolve negativities that may still be controlling us and to restore our divinity back into our physical lives. As we are ready AA Raziel will aid us to restore our ancient knowledge and put it into service to assist life to keep evolving. He knows when our vibration has reached a level that is ready to be taken up into our next stage of ascension. He will assist us to part the veils of unconsciousness, allowing divine knowledge to awaken us. One message of his is that we must be prepared to let go of about 90% of our past conditioning to allow for a new vision and unfoldment of self and life to occur. As this occurs, our environment shifts alongside of us, lifting into a higher vibrational reflection of creation. Our awakened divine knowledge assists with this as we are guided by Raziel to find new and exciting ways to express our creativity, ultimately becoming god infused co- creators of heaven on earth.

AA Raziel will assist people involved in work to do with ritual, psychic and spiritual healing and guidance. He will assist these healers to access the hall of knowledge to not only clear old karmic patterns but also to awaken and remind us of our light and spiritual expression.

Third-Eye Crystals

Amethyst works well at the third-eye as well as the crown chakra. The violet colour assists with the transformation of denser energies allowing you to see more clearly. The wonderful energy of this stone opens the clairvoyant vision and assists one's intuition to be clear allowing for a good healthy psychic system. Her action is strong and gentle all at once, giving one a sense of peace and trust in one's psychic skills. Use at the third-eye when doing manifestation visualisations as the energy of amethyst will expose and dissolve blockages to your desires.

Apophyllite. This stone is watery and feminine in nature. She nurtures the third-eye chakra, expanding one's understandings and visions. Her watery nature washes away old karmic ties and programs that may be hindering your growth. This then allows the growth of wisdom and understanding that apophyllite can activate. Apophyllite will also clear past life scars and heal and clear your emotional body.

Lapis Lazuli. I always feel so connected to Isis and ancient Egypt when I hold Lapis. This is a visionary stone and one that enhances any magical working. Lapis is made up of three main parts: lazurite, calcite and pyrite. With this blend she is able to break down old programs opening new visions and concepts that correspond to the individual's soul plan. She sees the truth and assists you to bring it into reality. Lapis strongly works with one's psychic abilities and the voice of knowledge and wisdom.

Azurite exposes untruths and reveals unconscious programs that are buried and hindering our ascent into wellness and wholeness. Her deep indigo ray penetrates deeply into the psychic potential and unconscious, marrying the gifts of the soul into a conscious action. Azurite has a warm and deep orange undertone which allows one's creativity to connect to the third-eye, not only revealing what's hidden health wise but also assisting with one's creative abilities.

Iolite carries pure indigo energy allowing it to be one of the strongest psychic activation stones available. Iolite works strongly with St Germaine and his violet ray. She helps dreams become realized and for action to be taken on situations that are revealed through her psychic visions.

Aquamarine has a cooling and cleansing effect on the endocrine system. We all need some revivification of these master glands from time to time as they work very hard for us. Most of them are constantly switched on, receiving and processing data just from our everyday lives. Aquamarine will soothe the pineal and pituitary glands, allowing through her watery nature for a clearer visionary experience.

Kyanite. I love Kyanite, actually I love them all but her action is so amazing on all levels. Kyanite seems to penetrate the light body, clearing, shielding and revealing what we need to know. She is like an ally that gets in there and takes care of business. Kyanite also deeply revivifies the endocrine system, bringing a much needed boost after a day of doing readings and healings. Kyanite works to marry the download of inspiration from the Source through one's mental body and brings it into usable information that we are able to work with. She also assists with telepathy and dream work.

Moonstone is the stone of the high priestess. It works to harmonise our hormones and boost our psychic sight. Moonstone enhances one's intuition and ability to have visions. She boosts our creativity, fertility and connection to emotions and the moon. Moonstone encourages intimacy and creative new beginnings.

Flower Essence – Third-Eye

Native Violet

Native violet is such a beautiful gift from the fairy realm. They are a small and dainty flower and emit a pure and innocent vibration. As you walk amongst the fields of flowers you feel transported into a different realm, a realm of magic and purity, the violet ray washing over you and lifting your vibration. One can sense unicorns and the tinkling of crystal waterfalls and fairy light just beyond the veil of one's perception.

Works with the third-eye chakra

Cooling and quieting to one's being, allowing one to receive intuitive knowing clearly

Good for children with behaviour problems, brings a balance to their brain, calming and soothing their organic reaction to an often over-stimulating environment

Visionary essence for artists and other creative pursuits, she assists medical intuitive healers to "see" without being taxed by the experience.

Clears unsettled energy in the aura and mind, allows for clear focus of ideas and manifestation magic

Brings problems into clear focus, assisting solution finding, lightening the load of worry

Brings in the fairy helpers to clear the way for rapid solutions to take place, they show you the way forward, linking your energy flow to theirs to recreate a positive outcome. The fairy beings are able to guide you through the astral illusions of unconscious creation and guide you swiftly to a positive outcome. A truly magical essence for recreating your future and envisioning outcomes.

Opens the way for wisdom and higher truths to come in.

Lavender Essence

Lavender essence works with St. Germain; it activates the violet flame of transmutation, assisting us to burn away unnecessary programs and energies that are no longer serving any higher purpose. Make it up with an amethyst crystal for added violet energy.

It works through time and space to clear old programs that may be sabotaging your success

Harmonises and heals the light body, healing any holes and leaking energy

Allows for clearer clairvoyance and intuition, clears psychic smog

Connects with the healing angels of the violet ray

Great for indigo and crystal children

Wonderful for nervous system healing

Lavender Rose Essence

Works with Lady Isis

Works with moon energy and the silver violet ray

Activates one's priestess energy and psychic awareness

Connects to the healing energies of Sirius and the whale, dolphin energies for DNA healing

Opens crown chakra to connect to akashic records, great for spiritual healers

Very cooling to the system, gives the endocrine system a lovely boost when dealing with high vibrational frequencies

Good for crystal and indigo children, helping them to feel at home and in touch with their angels and soul family

Essential Oils for Third-Eye Chakra

Lavender is a wonderful balancer, whether we are anxious, in need of upliftment or a nice cleansing, lavender will bring all levels back into harmony. This works well with the third-eye as an overload of information and sensory experience can cause a wobble in our nervous system and light body. A drop or two on the forehead or crown will bring a harmonious balance and integration back in. We need this balance in order to be able to operate our clairvoyance.

Sandalwood works well at all our centres. She is grounding, balancing and supportive to us living our spiritual life in an integrated physical way. She greatly enhances our meditation, bringing a deep peace and spiritual opening. This beautiful oil will strengthen your personal boundaries which are so important to this centre as you need to know what is your energy and what is another's. Sandalwood enables us to see with clairvoyant vision yet not take the energy into your system. This makes sandalwood a priceless oil to have.

Rosemary is so instantly cleansing and uplifting. She stimulates the endocrine system bringing in a lovely freshening of your energy. Her scent assists the mind to clear and to remember what is necessary and filter away what is not yours. Rosemary will promote clear thoughts, insight and understanding. She makes a great room mist for clearing and purifying your space.

Bay Laurel essential oil assists us to have visions. Rather that putting it directly on the third-eye, burn it in an oil burner and allow the fragrance to stimulate your clairvoyance. She assists with psychic protection so that you see clearly, releasing mental blocks so that new wisdoms can be accessed. This allows us to create new realities rather than have them blocked by old thought patterns that limit our reality.

Clary Sage enhances our dreams, allowing us to access information we may need in our dream state. She is a calming oil and has a slightly euphoric effect on our nervous systems. As we relax we are better able to reach into those theta states of consciousness where we are able to meditate and receive guidance. Clary sage will assist one to see what is hidden and bring it to light.

Peppermint is very purifying, the menthol effect cleansing and opening the third-eye. Not so much a visionary oil, more a cleanser so that the vision is pure - this is so important here. Polluted energy will not produce clear seeing; rather it may attract lower frequency images that can cause confusion and wrong guidance. This is oil is best diluted with some carrier oil and used on the back of the head, at the point where the head and neck connect. This cools and clears your personal channels.

Ritual of Activation for the Third-Eye Chakra and Light Code 10

A deep purple candle

Sage or frankincense to clear space

Chosen oil for chakra and candle

Third-eye sigil…AA Raziel

Chosen crystal

Third-eye essence for brow and to take internally

Smudge space to purify

Say prayer of protection

Place candle in a safe container with sigil under container or drawn on candle

Anoint candle with oil

Place crystal on self or next to candle

Take a couple of essence drops

Put yourself into a relaxed state, play soothing music, breathe deeply releasing tension and bringing your focus inward to what you are about to do for yourself.

Invoke AA Raziel

"In the name of love and light I ask my guides, celestial helpers and Archangel Raziel to please open, activate and balance my third-eye chakra, placing within it the crystalline structures and sacred geometries I need to fully bring my third-eye chakra into its highest vibration and health activation. I ask that the corresponding Light Code 10 and DNA be brought into perfect harmony with my soul's highest expression now. I command the activation of the 10th Light Code now, bringing it into its highest level of presence on every level of my light body and beingness. I am so grateful for this healing, thank you, Om Mani Padme Hum."

Feel the energy rising through your body, being drawn up into the third-eye region. There is a warm pulse of indigo light filling your head and spreading throughout your body, waves of energy and sensation lifting you up and into a deeply peaceful and receptive state. Your body feels a surrendering to this heavenly light, the indigo ray purposefully moving through out your body clearing and restructuring you on a deep and cellular level. You can feel the angelic support and the presence of your guides, guiding the energy and lifting the veil of forgetfulness from you. As the pineal gland fills with this energy a sense of rejuvenation fills you as the death hormone begins to become disabled and a new sense of self and potential is activated.

Do this activation and meditation as frequently as needed.

The seed sound for this chakra is OM.

Chant this to balance and energise your third-eye.

Animal Totem

The owl

The animal totem for this chakra is the owl. The owl sees in the night, they sleep through the day and take flight at night. They use inner sonar to direct their flight through the darkness. They teach us to trust our instincts, listen to our intuition and how to see what is hidden, what is still hiding in the unconscious and what the hidden meaning maybe within certain situations that arise. The owl can guide us through the realms of psychic understanding, giving us wings to fly through a misty environment and come out the wiser and stronger for having the courage to do so. Listen to owl when you need an understanding or insight to a question, he will help you see the truth. The owl is often associated with St. Germain, a sign that he is watching over you and responding to your prayers.

St. Germain

St. Germain is an ascended master; he achieved a state of immortal presence, living for over 300 years. There are testimonials from royalty in the 18th century that tell of his magical elixirs that assisted others to retain their youthful vitality. Part of his gift to the earth is the Violet Flame of Transformation. You can call on this flame to help you clear and heal as you work your way towards your own truth and liberation. This violet flame will be of great help in keeping yourself clear on all levels. As it is a violet ray it feels appropriate to include it here.

Violet Flame Invocation

"I call upon beloved Saint Germain

To instigate the Violet Flame of transformation and holy restoration

Please fill my body of light, my surrounding environment

With the purifying and powerful violet flame

Every cell and molecule of my being

Past, present and future

I AM now healed and cleansed by this holy flame

Restored into a state of abundant good health and well being

Thank you and so be it."

Use when you need a clearing and some support. Works very quickly, leaving you feeling connected to your pure lightness of being.

Mantra for Third-Eye Empowerment

Tara

Tara, Buddhist goddess of pure sight and presence:

"Om Tare Tuttare Ture Swaha"

(Om Tah-rei Too-tah-rei Too-rei Swah-hah)

"Om and salutations to She (Tara) who is the source of all

Blessings"

White Tara bestows rays of light, gives deep peace and bestows divine creativity and a long life.

Goddess Work

We will work with Isis, White Buffalo Calf Woman.

Isis is known as an Egyptian goddess, she is one of the most well-known goddesses today. There are layers to her teachings but eventually she was considered a goddess of life and universal wisdom. She is a moon goddess, working with motherhood, psychic awareness, magic and healing. Her ultimate learning about healing took place when her love, Osiris, was dismembered and scattered by a jealous companion. She found all the missing parts of Osiris and fooled the god Ra into telling her the sacred words for resurrecting life. She became the first woman to perform such a sacred task and as such was initiated as a priestess of very high degree.

Our workings with Isis will be around psychic awareness and magic. To start with we will make an incense to create a clear and psychic enhanced space.

Then using tarot or oracle cards, do a reading to look into some situation in your life you would like further insight into.

Using the cards you will observe what the past influences are, how they are affecting the present moment and how these energies that are formulating around you will show in a future outcome.

This is the potential outcome based on the direction your unconscious and conscious intentions and programs are leading you towards. As we have seen not all future outcomes are set in stone. They are a result of your vibrational magnetic frequency, what it is that you maybe unconsciously manifesting.

If the outcome card is not as you would like it to be, look through your cards and find a card that does resonate with your desired outcome.

Take this desired outcome card and place it on your altar and allow it to become your focus of desired intent. We do not have to be victims of outcomes that no longer serve us. Create the outcome you want, using the tools provided to recreate your desired reality.

Magical Psychic Reading

You will need:

A pack of tarot or oracle cards. Reading cards make a great focus for magical manifesting. They have years of magical lore and work within their blueprint of creation. This provides a bank of energy that is drawn upon to assist their purpose.

A violet candle

Isis's sigil drawn on candle or if you have the Isis sigil card place it under candle or crystal

An essential oil and crystal (lapis lazuli is great for working with Isis) from list provided in this section

Incense: either a good quality bought one or make your own. This can create an atmosphere that supports your visionary skills

Start this magical working just after the new moon; you will be adding energy to it every night until the full moon to build the energy and power of your intent.

Recipe for incense

Home-made incense is burnt on a charcoal block bought from a reliable stockist of incense materials.

Pinch of dried mugwort, a powerful psychic enhancer

Some frankincense resin, spiritually uplifting and purifying

Pinch of sandalwood powder, calms and creates a receptive space

Pinch of dried bay leaf as a psychic energiser

Mix a little of one of the recommended essential oils into it to bind and make it smell nice

Mix and grind them together, running your fingers and intent through the mix. When ready place some on a lit charcoal incense block and allow the smoke to cleanse, protect and spiritually uplift your sacred space.

This incense mix also makes a great blend to store your psychic working crystals in.

Say a prayer of protection and/or cast a magic circle of protection around you by seeing a blue circle of light surrounding your personal working space.

Get a clear idea of what your question or goal is for doing this reading.

Say an invocation to Isis:

"Isis of the full moon light

Please assist me with my psychic sight

Opening my spiritual eye

So that I can see my path of truth

Bringing me guidance and sacred visions

Magically guiding me to my highest mission." v

Shuffle your cards, concentrating on your question

Pick out three cards, laying them in a straight line

They represent, from left to right, the past, the present and the future.

Allow yourself a moment to relax, to get into a state of receptive listening. Soften your gaze and allow the cards to speak to you. What are the images and colours saying to you? Look at the characters and symbols on each card and see how they relate to your query.

When you are feeling ready, consider the future card, is this the future you would like to see? If not, look through the card deck and select a card that better suits your desired outcome.

Pack the other cards up and place the outcome card on your altar. Place the candle, Isis's sigil, crystals and any other sacred objects you feel enhance this working on the altar also.

Pick a green crystal from the heart chapter or an orange from the sacral chapter as they are good energisers for your manifestation card. Place the crystal on the tarot/oracle card.

Each night leading up to the full moon light your candle and as you look at your desired outcome card visualise your favoured outcome as having already occurred.

Command that this be so, remember you are moving the tides of energy to flow in a new direction so really put your intent and desire into the vision.

You can invoke Isis each night to help you as you work your magic.

When the full moon night is over release your magical working by giving thanks to the powers that be, release the magic circle of light and place the card and other objects back and release the magic, letting go of how your desired outcome will occur and instead just knowing that it will.

"Thank you Isis and blessed be."

White Buffalo Calf Woman

White Buffalo Calf Woman is a beautiful Native American holy woman who comes to teach humankind to revere spirit through honouring Mother Earth. She appeared to two young Indian men in a pillar of light. Her purity consumes evil and transmutes it to ash. One of the young men disappeared; her light was too strong for him. The other survived and went on to tell her story and spread her peace. She carries a reverence for all life and shares her teachings through sacred ritual. Through her peace pipe and medallion of the four directions (medicine wheel) she imbues life with her light and peaceful ways.

Medicine Wheel

The medicine wheel is a wonderful template to use when considering how to construct a ritual or sacred space. The wheel embraces the four directions and the four elements which all come together as a pathway of growth and wholeness. When we wish to create a ritual for a specific reason there are often many elements at work. There may also be unconscious lessons and blocks that can hinder the successful outcome. This is why many do not have success with their manifesting rituals; unconscious hindrances, not enough passion and fire in their intent or maybe a muddled mind and focus. The medicine wheel can help us create a balanced and reverent structure for healing, learning and creating.

I have taken the structure of the medicine wheel and adjusted it to fit in with simple ritual work. I was given guidance in this and have followed through with the following structure. All ancient knowledge is held in sacred space; we do not interfere with it but re-interpret it so that it can fit into a changing world, bringing the sacred into all that we do. I live in the southern hemisphere - if you live in the northern hemisphere you may want to reverse the directions. This is a very simplified version of the medicine wheel, created to help us learn to understand the structure of creation in our rituals and sacred work.

Here is a description of the meaning of the four directions and how to utilise them in your rituals. This is brief and simple. I like simple but you can study the wheel as there is so much more to learn.

East:
The wheel is entered through the east. This is represented by the element of air and speaks of beginnings, the idea, your vision and the intent of your ritual.

Elemental: Sylphs

Archangel: Raphael

Symbol: incense, feather

Crystal: citrine, clear quartz, amethyst, turquoise

Herbs: lavender, lemongrass, peppermint, sage

North:
We then travel to the north, the place of fire. This is our passion, creativity and inner child. This is the action we take to manifest our vision.

Elemental: Salamanders

Season: Summer

Archangel: Michael

Symbol: candle

Crystal: amber, carnelian, red jasper, ruby, sunstone

Herbs: allspice, angelica, basil, cedar, cinnamon, dragon's blood, frankincense, marigold, orange

West:
The west is the place of water. This is our emotions and unconscious, the place where we nurture ourselves and clear our unconscious blocks to achieving our successful outcomes. Look inward and create healing, allow the unconscious to dissolve its resistance to change.

Elemental: undines and mermaids

Season: Autumn

Archangel: Gabriel

Symbol: water, essences, shells

Crystal: aquamarine, calcite, coral, jade, moonstone, pearl, ocean jasper

Herbs: apple blossom, catnip, coconut, cyclamen, jasmine, lotus, peach, thyme, valerian, vanilla

South:
This is the place of the earth element. Here we manifest our desires on a physical level. We ground ourselves and embody our goals. We create an abundance of all things positive.

Elemental: Gnome

Season: Winter

Archangel: Uriel

Symbol: salt, crystals

Crystal: amazonite, aventurine, brown agates, emerald, jet, malachite, moss agate, petrified wood, smoky quartz, tigers eye, black tourmaline

Herbs: Cyprus, geranium, honeysuckle, mugwort, oak moss, patchouli, vervain, vetiver

Any of the correspondences can be used on an altar layout of the wheel. For example, at the *east* you could have a sprinkling of peppermint with a citrine crystal on it to usher in new ideas and energy. Your ideas will be protected and amplified into the universe.

At the *north* you would then light a red or orange candle and dress it in an oil to bring passion and oomph to the intention.

At the *west* a bowl of water with an appropriate essence for nurturing (peach) or healing and maybe place a crystal in the bowl to suit your needs.

At the *south* place a good grounding crystal like aventurine for success with a sprinkling of salt for protection of your intent.

In the centre of the wheel place a short written account of your intent, maybe a sigil over the top or a crystal.

That's it. Leave it for a week, giving it some energy and love to hold its focus and power.

A candle can be dressed with a chosen oil at each of the directions to enhance and work with those energies.

There are many ideas here on how to make your ritual your own.

There is a medicine wheel template provided or a coloured, laminated copy can be ordered.

Start each ceremony with a smudging and honouring of the four directions.

A circle call

"I cast this circle in the name of love and light and to create protection on all levels of my sacred space

I create a space beyond all time and space a temple of perfect grace

Where I can meet with my guides, angels and masters in peaceful union

Powers of the East, I call upon the element of air and the Archangel Raphael,

Keeper of healing mysteries and clear visions, hail and welcome

Powers of the North, I call upon the element of fire and Archangel Michael

Keeper of the warrior energy of protection and the lightning sword, hail and welcome

Powers of the West, I call upon the element of water and Archangel Gabriel

Keeper of the heart and emotions, hail and welcome

Powers of the South, I call upon the element of earth and Archangel Uriel

Keeper of the earth's magics and gifts of the land, hail and welcome."

Always close the circle when you are finished as this grounds the energy:

"I give thanks to the powers of the south, west, north and east,

Thank you and blessings as I release you back into the universe."

In the centre of the coloured one is an OM symbol to symbolise the fifth element which is ether or spirit. The OM is the seed sound of creation; this is surrounded by the sacred lotus, bringing everything up into spiritual paradise.

Summary of Light Code 10

As we can see this light code is very much about activating and embodying our clear sight, clear intent and co-creative abilities. We are switching on our creator god codes; these have several levels and higher activations yet to go, each one requiring even purer and clearer beingness. We are learning and discovering who we are and just what we are capable of, being in truth with ourselves and others, being one of the touchstones of this initiation.

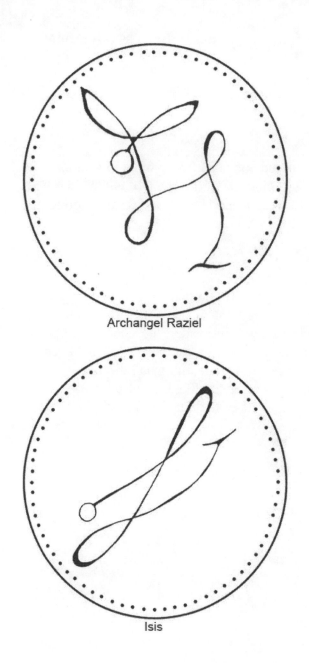

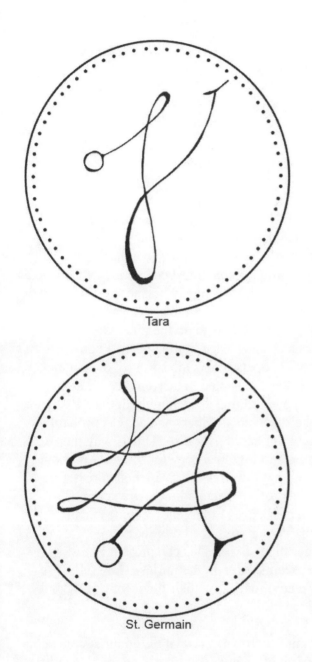

Chapter 8

Crown Chakra - Sahasrara

DNA Light Codes 11 and 12

Archangel Michael

The crown chakra is found on the top of the head. The main gland associated with this chakra is the pituitary. Other body parts connected are the cerebral cortex and central nervous system. Malfunctions can include depression, confusion, apathy, learning difficulties, stress overload and sleep issues. Over use may indicate someone performing too much psychic work which leads to imbalance in the other chakras. A nicely balanced crown chakra allows us to receive divine guidance and love, a clear knowing of what is (claircognizance) and access to divine gifts. One is at peace with themselves and their place in life. When a baby is born their crown chakra is wide open, this is the soft spot or fontanel. These little ones are still so connected to heaven - ever watched how babies are looking and smiling at seemingly nothing? Not so, they are still seeing their heavenly helpers and angels, probably family members who have passed over also. This is why the baby needs a lot of protection and loving energy for the early part of their life, they are so open. Flower essences applied here before going out is a lovely way to give them a little extra support. Australian Bush Flower Essences Emergency Essence is an excellent choice. Some young ones keep their heavenly connection open longer than others. This can present as a slow learner or a child who seems off with the fairies. They fully incarnate as they are ready; just enjoy their innocent beauty and support them as they are.

The crown literally is like a crown, a crown of light that connects us to our higher selves and the universal matrix of creation. We are connected to Source and so are flowing with truth and knowing of our life, where to go, what to do, what works and what is complete. Worry, stress and what-ifs have faded from our program, we just know and so just flow. The crown is often depicted as an ultraviolet lotus surrounded in golden white light. This is a wonderful image, assisting us to keep our airways open and in a high state of frequency so that we can stay in tune with our angels, guides and universal consciousness. This lotus has a thousand petals, each one connecting to infinite portals of knowledge and love. To fully understand the complexity of this chakra would be quite overwhelming. Every thought sends ripples through the stillness of our perfection. Stillness is the seed sound of this chakra, blessed silence so that the fine and delicate matrix can stay in tune with your higher direction and soul. Meditation is the key to strengthening this divine portal, meditation trains the mind to embrace stillness; practice will make this easier to achieve. When in deep meditation we can reach states of divine bliss, even a state of deep relaxation can unwind a stressed system. In this state our vital glands will secrete a nourishing fluid that revivifies our system, rejuvenating us on every level. When very high states of Samadhi are reached a fluid called amrita is released from the higher glands and this is the elixir of life, very sweet and nourishing on every level. So a lot goes on in the silence of the mind and crown chakra, much that we have yet to fully understand and achieve in our western style of living but I believe we can achieve these states of being and then extend and enjoy our lives in a more energised and full way.

From the crown chakra we learn to transcend time and space: all is now and we embrace all that we are and live it now. Our brains are instruments of awareness, a gift of access to our complete knowingness of the truth of life. They are a way to become an embodiment of pure spiritual connection, living with a connected flow to our spiritual inspiration. As we clear our programming and limitations we can access the limitless, it lives within every cell of our body. Through our crown chakra we can be human and limitless all at once. As we become reconnected to our cosmic consciousness we can access mysteries and secrets of the universe and of immortality.

Light Codes 11 and 12

"I AM Divine Wisdom" really encapsulates the energy of these light codes. You are now awakening and embodying your true spiritual wisdom, living it and allowing it to guide your life. We are infinite intelligence and are now accessing this within ourselves for the first time in eons. There is an aspect of our inherent divine mother and compassion energy embedded in this layer, a receptive gene that draws this divine universal vibration into us enabling us to experience and see life through this light. It is like this compassion sits at our crown filtering all that does not resonate with this love, assisting us to see with eyes of compassion, thus protecting us from harsh energies. Up until now it has been a masculine dominant society but now this divine feminine energy is waking up in all of us. Stuff is happening to awaken this code, to clear blocked grief and allow the feminine energy and emotional feeling state to become more acceptable. So see this receptive feminine compassion awakening in every cell, adding its divine energy to the matrix, evolving all your body functions, of being bathed in love, receptive goddess energy filtering all good things into your life on every level.

Archangel Michael

AA Michael comes to assist us with vanquishing the ego. "He who is like God" or "I AM Presence" are terms or names that describe him. He cuts through the veils of illusion with his mighty sword, revealing truth and wisdom. His sword will clear confusions and situations that confound us as we heal and move towards our liberation. Michael is often called upon as the divine protector, his royal blue mantle around our shoulders deflecting negative energies from interfering in our space and lives. I often feel sovereignty around AA Michael's energy; he carries such an illumined presence and a divine authority. He works with leaders and the law to assist in the upholding of not only our earthly laws but also the universal laws so that our creative evolution can occur with limited interference. I was once told that the police department is an aspect of AA Michaels work; note the colour of their uniforms. He is a warrior angel who fights for all that is good, honourable and righteous.

We can call on him when ever we need some protection and support in difficult situations. He is also called on to cut the cords of attachment that no longer serve us, even through time and space. When relationships end, difficult karmic lessons have been learned or it is time to move on to new experiences and chapters in life, call on AA Michael to cut the cords to free up your energy so you can truly move on without being drained by old situations calling you back in. His light is so valuable to us, I have him at the crown chakra so that he can protect and uphold our light and connection to the universe and the All that is. He will protect our right to be and our crown of stars that links us to our soul and perfected beingness.

Crown Chakra Crystals

Crystals can assist with your meditation practice and to keep your channels clear, energised and open to receiving guidance from your angels, guides and the masters who wish to help us on our journey.

Amethyst: The violet shades of amethyst work to transmute any interference with the finer frequencies of the crown chakra. She works with the violet flame, each empowering the other to work more effectively. Amethyst will guard the door of your crown ensuring you draw in positive and high vibrations to enrich your spiritual life.

Elestial Quartz Crystal: Elestials are said to have been brought into our world by the angels. The multiple points on these crystals represent the angelic realm and their points of light they use to connect to us and help us to heal and channel their energy and that of the masters. It tends to expose then offer assistance to clear what is interfering with your higher connections and consciousness. The elestials hold many ancient memories that can activate your own soul memories and cellular healing. Good for writers and other creative souls as it can activate their own memories and gifts which are then translated into their work.

***Lepidolite**:* This lovely violet stone contains lithium mica. Lithium assists the brain's hemispheres to balance and is used by chemists in brain balancing medications. Lepidolite will balance out emotions and intense mood swings. Generally she is about bringing balance and harmony. Do not put this in water as the lithium content will leach into the water. This stone soothes the inner critic who undermines our belief in what we receive spiritually.

***Clear Quartz**:* clear quartz is like a dose of pure light. Quartz will amplify other crystals, provide a boost to your light body and clarify and intensify your intent. Clear quartz can be programmed also to provide different services for you. For example, to empower your connection to guides or provide protection. She helps with DNA healing and cellular turn over. Quartz keeps the light body clear; she moves the light and energy assisting no stagnation to build up. Clear quartz is great to use in any essence making as she amplifies the healing energy of the other stones.

***Mother of Pearl**:* mother of pearl is included as she has the most wonderful array of ethereal colours that swirl through her surface. These colours connect you into the higher dimensions, they are translucent and full of movement and light. The angelic realms love these shells and the goddess energy is uplifted and brought into a state of grace and peace.

***White Rainbow Moonstone**:* once again we have the wonderful array of ethereal rainbow colours. These ethereal colours connect you to the angels and masters for telepathic communication. They will also bring into alignment all your subtle bodies, balancing the healing rays within your own light body. When using or wearing these precious stones you will find your psychic gifts become more sensitive and heightened. Just make sure you are in an environment where you feel comfortable to be in a heightened state. Not the best stone to wear shopping, too much chaotic energy flies around shopping centres and public places, best saved for doing spiritual work and ritual.

Flower Essence for Crown Chakra

Apple Blossom: Included in the apple blossom essence is mother of pearl, quartz and petalite. These crystals work beautifully to enhance and uplift the energy of this chakra. The apple blossom is a Venus tree and thus connects you into the fields of love and light that permeate our galaxy.

Works to balance the crown chakra

Opens one to the fullness of universal love, connecting to divine diamond light and grounding it into physical life.

Being such a Venus essence she connects to the angelic realms for communication and receiving love.

Attracts high souls when trying to conceive, assisting them to settle into your energetic space.

Commitment essence to renew life force of union or to start a marriage. Also helps you commit to a new project, drawing on universal forces of manifestation to infuse your situation with pure pranic life force to ground it into the earth plane.

What does not resonate with love shall be cleansed away.

Allows true inner beauty to shine thus attracting the blessings of the universe.

Makes a wonderful room mist to attract angelic energy into your home and work place.

Use in a ritual for planting seeds of love or a naming/commitment ceremony. Place some drops in a goblet and have the couple share the liquid as they say their vows or place on babies crown as an anointing fluid.

Mulberry Essence: Mulberry essence is the indigo child's essence (or indigo adult!). It balances the brains hemispheres bringing some equilibrium in for them.

These heightened beings are so quick and sensitive that everything becomes too much, this essence sorts the incoming data for them.

It will also assist in blood sugar balance allowing the endocrine system to sort the speed and assimilation of sugars for them.

Clears the pathways of the brain enabling them to see clearly their unique gifts and visions of life.

Mulberry will clear the psychic smog allowing truth to be experienced. This leads to a trust in self's knowing and an ability to stay true to self.

Helps the pancreas to handle the higher vibrations and psychic energies with out causing sugar spikes and hypoglycaemia.

In her action upon us she ameliorates grief and guilt issues allowing the sweetness of life to return.

Essential Oils for Crown Chakra

Frankincense*:* some of these oils will be repeated for the higher chakras as they work on multidimensional levels. Frankincense is a tree resin and one of the gifts from the wise men to baby Jesus. Its aroma heightens spiritual awareness and is a great meditation scent. It is said to deepen our breath and lift our vibration and awareness into higher states. She will connect us with the divine, within and with out. Can be burnt as incense or applied as anointing oil to third eye and crown chakras.

Sandalwood*:* sandalwood releases the mind from the constraints of the limited mind, expanding us into a relaxed embrace of the spiritual potential. She will bring you into the present moment, freeing you from the past thus allowing for deep spiritual experiences. Sandalwood is quite grounding and uplifting so makes a valuable ally in one's spiritual journey.

Rosewood: rosewood is often used in mala beads as it is a very spiritual wood. Rosewood will monitor how much spiritual growth we can safely embrace, she acts like an energetic filter, allowing a gentle and steady stream of heightened love to enfold us and carry us lightly back into a state of source-full connection. Too much kundalini energy too soon can burn our sacred chakra centres and potentially cause deep harm, rosewood nurtures our spiritual connection and plugs us into our higher self and universal guides safely. Used diluted in a massage oil will free up and loosen the kundalini energy when used along the spine.

Rose: rose vibrates at such a high frequency that she will always lift your vibration and connect you to higher masters and guides. By working on the heart energy with the rose oil you will open the gates of receptivity to higher states of consciousness, allowing your higher self to become more comfortably integrated into your physical life. Rose oil is expensive but even in its diluted state it is still very valuable oil for healing. The oil permeates the wound at an energetic level and carries it into a higher vibration where it just dissolves in the light of truth and unconditional love. Rose oil is wonderful for working with goddess energy, angelic love and the divine healing light of Mother Mary.

Ritual of Activation for Crown Chakra and Light Codes 11 and 12

A white or lavender coloured candle

Frankincense incense to clear and uplift the space

Chosen oil for candle and chakra anointing

Crown chakra sigil … AA Michael

Chosen crystal

Crown essence for spritz bottle and/or taking

Smudge space with your frankincense resin or oil in a burner or added to a spritz bottle

Say prayer of protection

Anoint candle with chosen oil

Place candle in a safe container with sigil either drawn on the candle or placed under container

Place crystal next to candle, hold it or place above head if lying down

Take a couple of essence drops

Put yourself into a relaxed state, play soothing music, take some deeply cleansing and relaxing breathes, releasing tension and day to day worries. Make an intention to accept this healing and activation for your highest good.

Invoke AA Michael

"In the name of love and light I ask my guides, celestial helpers and Archangel Michael to please open, activate and balance my crown chakra, placing within it the crystalline structures and sacred geometries I need to fully bring my crown chakra into its highest vibration and health activation. I ask that the corresponding Light Codes 11 and 12 and DNA be brought into perfect harmony with my soul's highest expression now. I command the activation of the 11th and 12th Light Codes now, bringing them into their highest level of presence on every level of my light body and beingness. I AM now connected into my higher self and soul's light, grounding them into my physical experience

and life expression. I am so grateful for this healing, to now have closer connection to my guides, masters and angels, to work as one in a state of harmony and peace. Om Mani Padme Hum."

Feel the state of peace and inner harmony coming into alignment within you. Allow the angels, masters and guides to work with you to instigate this wonderful healing and coming home. You feel lifted into a state of wholeness, full of light yet quite present in your body. Hold this energy; feel into the sense of connection that is occurring now, becoming an embodiment of your true self, of grounding all of this magnificence into your daily life. Your mind is in a state of deep calm and peace, no more room for worry or separation from that which you are. The pineal and pituitary glands are being rejuvenated and are spilling their vital fluids into your system, causing a deep healing and resurrection of your spirit. Know and feel this to be so and so it shall be.

The seed sound for this chakra is silence. In the silence all that is can be so, just allow yourself to be silence, soak it in and connect into universal oneness.

Animal Totem

Eagle

Eagles have always been symbolic of Great Spirit, soaring high above the worries of the world. The eagle sees the bigger picture and assists us to escape the limiting ego's version of events and carries our mind into higher states of consciousness, allowing us to transcend 3D existence and enter into a closer relationship with the Great Spirit that resides within us all. As we learn to embrace this higher vision we shall ascend into even greater states of heightened awareness. The eagle embraces the silence and stillness of being, he flows in a state of oneness with creation, knowing that all is well just as it is. Invoke Eagle's assistance to see above the emotional reactions of life and to become one within a state of equilibrium, knowing that in your stillness all shall be understood.

Mantra for Crown Chakra Empowerment

"Om Trayumbakam Yajamahe

Sughandhim Pushti Vardanam

Urvar-ukamiva Bandhanan Mrityor

Muksheeya Mamritat."

(Om try-um-bah-kum ya-jahm-mah-hay

Soo-gahn-dim poosh-tee vahr-dah-nahm

Oor-vahr-oo-kumee-vah bahn-dahn-ahn

Mrit-your mook-shee-yah mahm-ree-taht)

"Shelter me, O three-eyed Shiva. Bless me with health and immortality and

Sever me from the clutches of death, even as a cucumber is cut from its creeper."

This mantra is helping us to dissolve our fear and programming around death. As we do this our vital glands and inner intelligence can restore our DNA back into a state of truth and inner auto-healing. Our body will be free to rejuvenate instead of reacting to an inner prompt from our cells which says it is now time to begin aging and dying. As we attain this timeless state of being, genetically inherited and karmically inherited diseases will just cease to be. They will lose their power and simply begin to deactivate. This mantra will help you heal and become attuned to a higher state of being and knowing. Even if death comes it is in a realised state of knowing that it is only a short nap and then life continues. A deep consciousness has been awakened and life now has a whole new understanding.

Goddess Work

We will work with Hathor, Egyptian goddess of love.

Hathor

Hathor originally came from Venus. She was actually born from a race of beings called The Hathors. They arrived on Venus many eons ago with the intention of assisting with the populating and educating of the people on Earth. Hathor was sent to earth, incarnating as the daughter of Ra, an Egyptian god. She came to help us become embodiments of love: she teaches pleasure, ritual, sensual and sacred sexual love. In working with her we can rise above the emotional entrapments love often leads us into and keep our loving energy clear and light, infused with spirit and higher states of consciousness.

A Message from the Hathors

"I AM, all things in your world revolve around the I-AMness of existence. In order to expand into the almighty I AMness of existence it is imperative that you immerse and embrace your true selves, your polarity of male/female balance and open your hearts so they can hear the songs of the ethers. As you do this and birth this truth back into your lives you shall become more and more in tune with God I Am, all things shall flow more comfortably for you, manifestation shall follow effortlessly and love shall blossom in all it many and varied ways.

Rejuvenation can be achieved in a similar fashion. Nature has all the answers. Learn to allow your heart to reach towards the nectar of its own knowing, the balance of its sun and moon and the source of all nourishment. Follow its leads and you shall find all that you need to keep yourself journeying towards your light and fulfilment. Doors open when you surrender the fight and survival, learn to just exist, acting in the moment, this takes so much strain off the body, mind and spirit. When the spirit is allowed to guide, the body receives all it needs to happily provide the means of support and action. When spirit guides, doors open miraculously, showing you the next step. Envision with you third-eye and feel from your heart that which you know lights up your being, what it is that excites you, feel it and allow spirit to take this heart transmission of yours and begin creating an appropriate physical experience of it for you. Your spirit knows you better than anyone else; it still has a pure connection to your soul and all the spirit helpers that surround you. This spirit knows what you are ready and able to embrace and the appropriate steps to assist you towards your goals in a comfortable and doable way.

As you learn to listen within your silence, you will start to strengthen, your clairvoyance and your intuition shall grow stronger, the polarity of your existence will unify, your essential glands will heal and lubricate your system and your light body will organically expand, embracing other realities and possibilities. This process is called ascension. You grow beyond the old structuring of this 3D reality and your DNA restructure back into the remembered hologram of your original wholeness. All you need to achieve this is all around you. Be still and it will make itself known to you, for the blessings of the natural world have their own consciousness and communication system. In the silence they will reach out towards your hologram with what you personally need, you will perceive this as you notice something that catches your eye and interest. In this way of being you learn to extend and rejuvenate yourselves for you are living in the flow of light from source rather than the drive of survival from the ego of mass consciousness.

This is truly the way of the goddess, she organically magnetises what she needs to sustain her love and light, to feed her fertility and creativity. Existence feeds itself, become the personification of your true goddess self, allow the universe to care for, to feed and love you for you are her expression of love."

"Fill yourselves from my Light

Extract the nectar of pure limitless wonder

Become my expression of inexhaustible love

Open thyself to limitless, sublime expression

Express through the heart centre of all seeing

And become an ocean of consciousness floating on the sea of love"

Hathor energy assists us to magnetise positive light towards us. This is especially helpful with the crown chakra as it draws benevolent and loving energies into us through our crown, maintaining a high vibration that filters out any darker energy that could interfere with your clear stream of light and connection to your higher self. We are learning to trust life again, to embody these finer energies and open ourselves like a flower to the supernal light of enlightened life.

Hathor energy also shows us how to experience sacred sexuality. When lovemaking is done consciously and with deep love and respect, it can build the light body and magnetise it to draw in more light and positive experiences to grow from. This type of lovemaking also builds the Ka body; this is a mirror image of our physical body. This is a very advanced teaching and probably not for now but the Ka body will also evolve your light body considerably and is one big step closer to teleportation and other spiritual gifts. Channelling sacred love is not hard, it just takes awareness and willingness between us to not fear the deeper sensations of love moving through our bodies. It is that feeling of vulnerability that can cause the contraction against these feelings. Read up on tantric practices to get an idea of how to begin freeing up the sexual energy from just the lower chakras and expanding the sexual love energy all through your body. It can be quite transcendental.

Ritual of Sacred Water

Sacred water is blessed water, charged water and holy water. Water can be imbued with energy; it takes on the imprint of the energy pattern of whatever is being used, whether it is sound, crystals, plants, chanting or prayer. Dr Masaru Emoto has written extensively on this, so read his work if you want more understanding. He provides photos of the change in crystalline patterning in the water when different energy is invoked; he illustrates the negative as well as the positive effects.

We will charge our water with Hathor energy. You can use it in many ways.

Place in your bath

Use as a base in a spritzer bottle

Make a large bottle and use it as your drinking water for the day

Water your plants

Place some in the ocean or other water bodies as a gift of healing to the earth

Blessings for babies or weddings

Wash your floors

Rinse your hair, giving your crown a good cleansing and uplifting

Place in a bowl on your altar, with a crystal in it for a specific condition or to represent water

Let your imagination run with ideas

Select crystals and oils from other chapters to add to your sacred water, enhancing and personalising the healing effect.

Call on Hathor for:

Fertility: drink the water to balance and enhance conception

Sacred love: attracting a partner or for making sacred love - use water in a spritzer with a favourite oil to enhance energy of room for love making or rinse hair to magnetize love towards you

Blessings: place on forehead of baby or drink from a goblet to infuse the marriage union with love and commitment

Beauty: wash face in water scented with favourite oil

Emotional balance: spray light body with lavender scented water

Healing: drink when under the weather; make an aura spray with a couple of drops of rose geranium to heal any weakness in aura and fill up with love

Prosperity: place a bowl of water on your altar with some aventurine in it to attract wealth

Spiritual light: drink water, wash hair with water and make a spritzer with neroli oil in it, anoint your chakras with a drop of blessed water and oil to cleanse and lift their vibration up

Make it under moonlight for feminine issues or under sunlight for more power and vitality

Instructions

A glass or crystal bowl

Clear quartz

Spring water

A candle with Hathor's sigil drawn on it

Hathor's sigil to place under your bowl

Sacred chant music, Tibetan bells or silence, whatever feels sacred to you

Place spring water in cleansed bowl

Say a prayer of protection or sacred circle invocation

Light your candle

Place cleansed clear quartz in water and any other cleansed crystal that assists with your intention

Place Hathor's sigil under your bowl of water

Say whilst holding your hands around the bowl:

"Hathor of the sacred light

Infuse me now with eternal life

Your heavenly presence is diamond bright

Your love is manna, heaven born

My cells, your cells

Our breath is one

Raise up the goddess within me now

Bring forth my radiance a prayer for all."

Blow a small breath into the water

If you have a crystal bowl make it sing to add amplification of energy

Or use your Tibetan bells or sacred chants. Silence is also very holy, whatever feels doable and works for you.

Sit in a meditative state as long as you wish, enjoy the peace and energy this ritual brings. You can leave the water overnight, a couple of hours or use straight away.

Your water is ready to use in whatever sacred way you had in mind.

It is good to lightly cover your bowl if leaving it overnight and it is also nice to create a sacred altar space to have your bowl set up in.

Close your circle and extinguish your candle when finished.

Summary of Light Codes 11 and 12

We are learning and becoming an embodiment of our true spiritual selves. Our window to the oneness of life is open and we are living in flow with our higher directives. We just know what we need to know and now embody that oneness throughout our body, through the energy vortices of our chakras. Each part of us is now supporting the other to create a wholeness and divine functionality that allows us to be co-creators with Great Spirit. Our ego works for us not against us, assisting us to be embodiments of divinity and yet function in our physical world. Your dream state maybe heightened with this activation, they may become more prophetic and contain messages helpful for your journey. As these codes become more adjusted and balanced you can experience a lovely sense of calm, just knowing all is well. It feels like coming home.

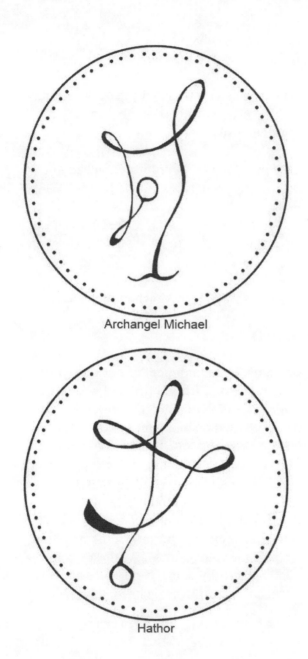

Chapter 9

Soul Star Chakra

Light Codes 13 to 24

Archangel Zadkiel

Receive and be guided by divine guidance, open channel to divine love, just know what you need to know. Over use can lead to migraines, tinnitus and general imbalance. Imbalance in this chakra can manifest as being in denial, may feel anger at 'God' or religion, unforgiveness and stress.

We are now reaching up into the holographic universe as we begin our journey through the transpersonal chakras. A hologram is an image of the whole, any part of the hologram, any section will contain everything. This is a big concept to understand but will hopefully make more sense as we go. Within the hologram of existence, no matter where you stand you are still a part of the whole. So let us break that down even further, no matter where you are in your spiritual journey as a human or spirit, you are still whole and a part of everything. Even if you are some murdering serial killer you are still a part of the heavenly hologram of wholeness, you are limited in how much of that hologram you can partake of as your vibration will keep you contained within the hologram. It is the vibrating frequency of your energy field that will decide how much of the hologram you are able to move in or ascend through. Raising our vibration through our rituals and aids such as meditation, essential oils, essences and one's thoughts all work towards raising one's frequency so that we may connect into more and more of the hologram. Within this hologram are layers of existence, dimensions that create a structure that we are able to work with. There are rays of colour and vibration that all sing into our energy bodies, teaching us and drawing us ever forward towards achieving a higher spiritual state. This is happening very quickly now as the earth herself is birthing as we as individuals birth towards a new position in our universal hologram. As we have seen, every cell in our body contains all our DNA and Light Codes. A blood test can tell us about any part of our body.

So what we are getting at here is that no matter who you are you are a complete aspect of the universe. These higher chakras are your link to all that you are, by healing our more physical aspects we can then raise our vibration and plug into that which we already are. All that we need to heal ourselves is already available to us through our gateway chakras. It is just a matter of knowing and believing that you are already God; no matter who you are you are still that part of the hologram of existence and have the potential to consciously connect back into this supreme intelligence at any time.

All the planets, seasons, rays, moon phases and tides have an effect on us. Our organs and physical wellbeing are all affected by these seemingly outer events. So as we work with our lovely gifts and tools we are continually reweaving our personal matrix. Bringing it into a closer and more cleanly unified field of light that connects us more easily to the master that we already are. Our fields of light will also enable us to connect more comfortably to the masters and angels for healing and knowledge and keep us aligned with our higher self and flow of pure potential.

The Soul Star is your quintessential connection point between the universal hologram and your own light body. Our Soul Star is who we are: it is our consciousness and blueprint of individuality within the oneness. It contains our gifts, karmic influences, talents. All that we have been, are and will be is contained within this starry chakra's body of light. When we incarnate we move down through the higher octaves of light and universal and soul consciousness. We then draw our awareness down through the cosmic gateway, Universal Gateway and Stellar Gateway until we draw ourselves into the Soul Star that then guides the incarnating soul/essence into the physical body through the chakras. The Soul Star retains all the memories we need as we lose our spiritual memory as we descend into physical expression. We become grounded as our elemental body separates out into earth, air, water and fire. By keeping these elements balanced within us we are able to more comfortably operate physically and enjoy the sensations of physical life. Often this sensation of separation and loss of memory can leave a soul feeling very homesick and suffering from low self-esteem. Once we realise we can never be lost, that we are an integral part of the universal oneness, then such spiritual afflictions will simply disappear and been seen for the illusion that they are. There is much to find pleasurable in our physical experience, it is safe to let go and let god as our Soul Star will keep us connected as we learn to dance our way through the delights of being alive.

Light Codes 13 – 24

Our Soul Star grounds into our Earth Star thus grounding our wholeness and potential into the earth plane. Thus our wholeness is alive in every cell and light code giving us the opportunity to evolve, access our gifts and operate on all levels. These two chakras really operate as one, each one supporting the other to keep us alive and connected to the hologram of all that is. They become our tube of light that runs through the centre of our body, delivering prana and life force to all our systems. It carries the soul's imprints, information and knowing throughout our systems, keeping us aligned and connected to our souls directives at all times. When this communication highway gets blocked and distorted by earth's lessons we can lose our health, feel disconnected from life and fee generally off track. There is a magnetic pull between these two chakras delivering vital information. When we work towards maintaining a clear and healthy pranic tube of light we find ourselves functioning far more effectively and in sync with our soul's directives. The colour associated with this chakra is ultra-violet. Imagine that colour vibrating throughout your light body, burning away all interference and impurities so that your precious soul's light can keep a steady and healing energy alive in your system, keeping you connected at all times.

Archangel Zadkiel

AA Zadkiel's violet ray works well with this chakra. Zadkiel represents divine compassion and comfort. This divine comforter energy supports us with unconditional love and protection. The protection is like a force field of light that helps filter our more negative thoughts and beliefs and prevents them from attracting in through our very refined chakras, any negative experiences and energies. These transpersonal chakras are so open to the divine and ethereal light that they can be impacted by thought very quickly; this is why we have limited conscious access until we have truly evolved ourselves into a strong and clear channel of love. Zadkiel supports and comforts our vulnerability and fragility. Do not see our learning as a weakness; we are loved for our willingness to go through this process of evolvement and the higher forces work with us as one to help us achieve this. It is ok to be vulnerable, to recognise your fears and imbalances; it is all part of embracing all that is and becoming a compassionate and loving being. As we learn to embrace and thus transcend our limitations, Zadkiel bestows on us limitless wisdom and clarity of spiritual vision that allows us to grow and expand into these higher vibrational fields of life. They become integrated as a part of us and our ascension; these higher chakras become consciously integrated into our unification of expression.

Zadkiel's energy is a continual flow of gifts and blessings. Our heart under his care shall open wide enough to overcome our self imposed obstacles and our spiritual muscle shall create the momentum to carry us into the divine flow of our creative source. No more limitations to our blossoming abundance, just pure potential and the fullness of joyful surrender.

During the times of Atlantis, Zadkiel's empathic energy blended with the energy of the divine mother, channelling her love directly from the galaxy. His violet ray works in with ritual as a way to connect to the divine and also as a connection to St. Germain and the Flame of Transformation. The violet ray assists to transmute the negative thought patterns we are ready to release, for they cannot release until we are ready, so Zadkiel protects us as we journey and understand the big picture and say "Yes, I am ready to let go."

Even though AA Zadkiel is stationed at the Soul Star, AA Metatron can be called upon to link this chakra to the Earth Star as AA Sandalphon and AA Metatron have a very close association. AA Metatron will be more closely looked at in following chakras.

Soul Star Crystals

Herkimer Diamond: the beautiful Herkimer is just a manifestation of pure, solidified spiritual light. They emanate a high vibrational energy that sings its way through all the chakras, holding this light true for us as we climb our spiritual ladder. They will help you communicate with angels and spiritual masters, attuning your energy to a true and supernal light octave. They assist in the removal of and dissolving of heavier energies and make a great tool for healers. Many have used them as an aid in astral travel and interdimensional work. Working with Herkimers will also help your psychic vision to open, stimulating the third eye, crown and etheric chakras. The Herkimer will increase the amount of light in the body thus displacing any diseased or heavier energy. They are good in an essence as they greatly assist the DNA to heal through connecting to the Soul Star and feeding our truth into and through our physical and spiritual bodies.

Drink Herkimer diamond infused water, then carry the crystal on you, having programmed it to correct any imbalance in your health and DNA programming, bringing your wellbeing into its highest state of evolvement. The crystal will then hold this truth for you as you transmute your health back into its optimal state.

Amethyst: dear amethyst again, as she connects to the violet light so well she is worth a mention again. She is so good for working with St Germain, AA Zadkiel and all things violet, transformational and spiritual. Amethyst will help you release those thought forms that AA Zadkiel is here to assist you to let go of. Use her in rituals of spiritual connect and of healing and release.

Labradorite: Labradorite is a stone of magic and awakening. The colours that shift and move so ethereally across her surface, connecting into the finer fields of light that surround us at all times but can be hard to attune into at times. She works magically with the violet ray of ritual as Labradorite is all about magic and shifting perspectives, giving us inner vision to truly "see" the truth and experience these higher fields of life. She will help us travel interdimensionally, experiencing and learning from other planes of existence and the masters who dwell there. This crystal is a magician's stone for she holds keys of learning how to enter the fields of pure potential and create our reality anew. Labradorite can show us the way through unseen realms, purifying and stabilising the path, protecting our light as we learn and experience new wonders.

Petalite: petalite is a pure heart centred crystal. She will transport you straight into the arms of the angels and divine mother energy. Petalite will open your psychic gifts, creating a connection with your heart to enable a pure and light infused visioning and healing. This is quite a strong crystal so she will assist you to ground your higher truths and longings, bringing them into physical reality for you. This works grandly with the Soul Star as this is what this chakra is all about. They make great companions.

Flower Essence – Soul Star Chakra

Indigo Iris

The Iris family are very angelic in their signature, the colours and delicacy of their form all contributes to a very celestial companion. She not only attracts angels but also highly evolved elemental devas who assist us to recreate ourselves, our world and all things beautiful. Iris is sometimes known as a goddess/angel of the rainbow, the colour spectrum of all the rays making her a truly majestic ally.

Works with Soul Star chakra, linking it into our Earth Star…think about the wonderful, juicy bulb buried in the earth from which they grow and bloom.

Opens our crown and upper chakras to a higher spectrum of colours and vibrations that live beyond our 3D environment.

Draws the angels and devas who travel on these currents of colour to lift our life force and help us fulfil our divine service.

Will assist souls who are passing to see their loved ones and angels, thus helping them pass into the light.

Helps with all life transitions such as starting school, puberty, marriage, divorce and new jobs.

Lifts sadness and depression, helping one to see the wonderment of life, opens one up to the flow of universal wisdom, healing the egos attachment to fear and loss.

As these concepts are embraced enlightenment can unfold.

Iris helps high souls step down as they prepare to incarnate into conception.

Clears the pranic tube, supports channellers to open and hold high vibrational energies.

Links the physical to the ethereal, heavenly body to physical self, manifesting heaven on earth.

Weaves a spiritual body out of light, adding and refining the light quota as we evolve. We become our ascended light body physical selves here on earth. This is one of the Soul Star's main functions.

Using essences will help keep these higher delicate chakras clear and luminous, cleansing psychic smog and mucus from clouding their function. These chakras are very responsive to the fine energies of vibrational essences. The essences strengthen and protect these finer energies so that they can remain open and healthy in our reality, sometimes they can be compromised by the denser experiences and places we go. Working this way allows us to remain light and open no matter the situation, not closing down in reaction to these times.

Essential Oils for Soul Star Chakra

Angelica: this is the oil of angels. Angelic attunes the brain to seeing life from a different perspective; she broadens the mind and assists us to see beauty in all things. She aligns the physical and inner eyes so that our vision rises in vibration so that we see the magic all around us. Angelica expands the heart and our ability to feel compassion towards our self and others. She will also strengthen the immune system, uniting lost parts and creating a greater sense of wholeness. Angelica restores health and stamina, our nervous system strengthens enabling more light to expand within us.

Grapefruit: grapefruit will cleanse the light body allowing for a clearer vision of yourself and how you relate to life, coming more from your souls directives rather than your egos. Grapefruit will lift depression making change that much easier to embrace, for life is continually ebbing and flowing as we evolve. This can at times overwhelm the system causing a bit of a shut down, grapefruit will assist the flow. She refreshes the mind and body, moving any stagnancy on physical and spiritual levels. This clearing and refreshment then puts us in touch with our psychic centres, allowing for an expansion of vision, realities and creative energy. Energetically grapefruit can remove karmic blueprints held in the etheric blood, thus clearing old thought forms from holding us back. Rubbed into the temples will assist clairaudience, used over spleen will work on karmic blueprints. Through all this work she connects us to the angel within.

Sandalwood: use sandalwood here to connect your Soul Star chakra to your Earth Star chakra. This unique oil works equally well at both, it grounds and uplifts at the same time bringing these two chakras into a magnetically harmonious flow of attraction. This keeps your etheric pranic tube flowing in a healthy and vibrant way, keeping all systems and chakras flushed with healthy, life giving energy and connection to your spiritual self.

Palmarosa: Palmarosa heals mother issues. Unresolved mother issues can interfere with our receptive side, receiving insights, opening spiritual gifts and connecting to the divine mother. These wounds can lead to a disconnection from our selves and eventually ill health. Palmarosa ever so gently reweaves our ethereal light, drawing down these feminine mothering forces to heal and support our upliftment into the fold of universal feminine love. When we anoint ourselves with Palmarosa it instils a sense of security that allows us to feel safe enough to open our wings and soar again. She is also very renewing on a cellular level which is great for facials or upgrading our DNA.

Ritual of Activation for the Soul Star Chakra and Light Codes 13-24

A white or violet candle

Sage or Frankincense to smudge

Chosen oil for candle and self anointment

Soul Star sigil … AA Zadkiel

Chosen crystal

Soul Star essence … take it and/or spritz it around light body

Smudge space to purify

Say prayer of protection

Place candle in a safe container with sigil either drawn on candle or placed under holder

Anoint candle with oil

Hold your crystal or place nearby

Take a couple of essence drops to put yourself into a relaxed state, play soothing music, breathe deeply releasing stress and tension, bring your focus inward to what you are about to do. Remember to disconnect phones and create a safe a quiet environment for yourself.

Invoke AA Zadkiel

"In the name of love and light I ask my guides, celestial helpers and Archangel Zadkiel to please open, activate and balance my Soul Star chakra, placing within it the crystalline structures and sacred geometries I need to fully bring my Soul Star chakra into its highest vibration and health activation. I ask that all the corresponding Light Codes, 13 through to 24 be brought into harmony with my soul's highest expression now. I command the activation of the 13th through to the 24th Light Codes now, bringing them into their highest level of presence on every level of my light body and beingness. I ask that all my Light Codes come into harmony with each other, each supporting the harmonious action of the other as a unified whole. I am so grateful for this healing, thank you, OM Mani Padme Hum."

Relax and allow the guides to assist this healing - no need to rush, just keep going into a deeper state of surrender. Experience every breath expanding the light through out your light body, feel the light above your head expanding until it encompasses your whole body, bathing you in the luminous waves of love from your soul. Take your awareness to your earthstar chakra, feel the pulsing ball of light, see streams of energy rising up through the core of your body, magnetically drawn into the ball of light above your head which is your Soul Star. As they connect a rainbow of light explodes around you, surrounding you then flowing down, magnetically drawn into your earthstar to begin the flow again. Do this several times to strengthen your pranic tube and earth and heaven connection.

Animal Totem

Butterfly

Beautiful butterfly, she makes a perfect totem for the Soul Star. She is so light and ethereal in her movements. She represents our ever changing self and evolvement. Every time we grow and transform ourselves we add new colours to our wings. These new colours represent the badge of initiation, another completed level of our ascension. We are continually returning to the chrysalis to reform ourselves, rebirthing a new and expanded sense of ourselves. Learn to be light and fluid like the butterfly, releasing the old and rebirthing a new and lovely aspect of self. Allow the colours to work with you, each ray a new learning and initiation into higher states of consciousness and awareness.

Mantra

This mantra is about fulfilling desires. Rather than using it to bring about untold physical wealth, it would be used for fulfilling the desires of the soul. It could be the soul wants a new car, that is great but understand it as a key into the Soul Stars link to your higher self and soul. Maybe it is like an access code to your higher directives guidance and by using this mantra you can create a greater connection and awareness of these higher centres. By all means use it to visualise a material need but also as a focus for wisdom and virtues you wish to grow within you. Using it this way you activate and work your higher centres, strengthening them so that your link grows clearer and stronger, making it more user-friendly in your physical life. You will notice that compassion enters into this mantra, compassion being one of the key words for this chakra's health and service.

"Om Kama Dayinyei Namaha"

(Om Kah-mah Dah-een-yei Nah-mah-hah)

"Salutations to She who is compassion itself"

The divine mother is the energy behind most mantras, her many names appearing to energise and focus their intent. One could say Lakshmi, Saraswati or Durga were part of the healing vibrations behind this mantra. It is lovely and will lift your heart up and open it to these divine celestial forces.

Hold an idea of your intent in your mind as you chant and allow the frequencies of sound to lift them up into the heavens for manifestation. Through song and sound we channel this divine light through our being and into the physical plane, infusing the environment with pure light energy. When we infuse our intentions with divine energy, an access code opens to allow our thoughts to enter into the flow of creation. Make a ritual of it by creating an altar with flowers, candles, incense and any other sacred objects you fancy. Become the frequency of love generated by these mantras and rituals and explore how they enhance your vibration, your life and wellbeing.

Goddess Work

Mother Mary

Mother Mary is best known as the mother of Jesus. She is also known as Lady Mary and Mary Queen of the Angels. It is obvious from these titles that she is a powerful aspect of the Divine Mother. Many have reported miraculous encounters with her and healers are often supported by her loving presence. It feels appropriate to work with her at this centre as she is the mother of compassion and will assist us to infuse our Soul Star with this loving light, not only helping our Soul Star to open but also to shield it through the compassionate love of the Divine Mother. This compassion acts like a filter, keeping our light body pure and open only energies of a higher frequency. This is important as these higher centres can only strengthen when we have mastered our minds, not entertaining negative or harmful thoughts.

Mary's Ritual of Diamond Light

This meditation/ritual is about opening the inner heart, bringing the divine into the earth. She teaches us how to develop the immaculate heart which is the same as the divine heart. As we develop this we shall be able to hold a vision of our inner perfection, which then extends its energy to humanity as a whole, embracing all as one. This then leads to envisioning the dream, the ideal way of being and creating our lives and that of our world, seeing a better vision continually unfolding for ourselves and for all.

Using a pink diamond we shall activate, plug in and secure our crystalline matrix of light that surrounds our light body. Our crystalline matrix encompasses all the layers of our immediate fields of light, protecting and energising them. It is shaped like a multidimensional diamond, with points at bottom, top and front, back and sides. The points at the front, back, sides, top and bottom all hold the outer edges of the light body in a secure, multidimensional framework, allowing for a transpersonal gateway to be resurrected, even in our day-to-day lives. As it is securely grounded in the Earth Star, you are safely anchored in your reality but able to operate with your higher self and council and become your evolving self with out continually compromising it to function in your day to day life. Being a pink diamond works on the spiritual heart, which is a key to safely unfolding your light body to embrace your wholeness.

Place either on your altar, in your meditation space or in a circle around you the following:

Have some rose essential oil or some rose geranium oil or palmarosa, all of which create a rosy atmosphere. Place some on yourself, in an oil burner and/or in spritzer and on candle.

Fresh roses or another favourite flower is always a complementary addition.

Pink candle with Mary's sigil drawn on it or under the candle holder.

Some rose quartz to place on your heart, or place near candle or in a circle surrounding you. This circle of crystals can be alternated with amethyst and clear quartz crystals.

Another idea would be to place your crystals in a diamond shape on your altar over a photo of you to hold the geometry of the diamond in place as it is going through its strengthen stage. Or place them in a diamond design around your body if you are lying down.

Say your prayer of protection before you start.

Then say:

"Divine Mary full of grace

Holy Mother, open my heart to your love

Morning star of light sublime

Through me manifest miracles

Dispelling darkness

Igniting the eternal flame of Christed wholeness

So paths become one

Unified in the sunlight of your holy presence."

Get into a comfortable and relaxed state, with gentle music and some deep breaths to deeply release any stress and to bring you into the present moment.

See a pink diamond in the very core of your heart. It is blazing with brilliance and intensity.

As the diamond starts to expand, smaller diamonds appear in every cell of your body, blazing their brilliance and twinkling like tiny stars.

The Mother diamond continues to expand until you are completely contained within her form.

Her points connect into the Soul Star chakra, the Earth Star chakra, a point out in front of you, behind you and to each side of you, anchoring your diamond symmetrically around you.

Feel your deep core heart expanding open and flooding you with love.

There are sparkling stars appearing at the six points on your diamond, these stars are connections to angels and guides who are helping you to anchor and activate your crystalline matrix.

Bring a rose into your awareness within your heart, allow it to fully bloom. When it is open, see it absorbing any old emotions or programs that may be holding you back at this time, old wounding and psychic injuries may also come up. When the rose has done its work, move it outside of your diamond space and blow it up, see it returning into heavenly light and lifting away.

Through the doorway of the diamond crystalline matrix, Jesus comes into the chamber of your heart and utters a blessing of love that expands throughout your being, connecting you into your own Christed essence.

See the diamond grow even more intense, its colours morphing as your soul directs its healing requirements for you.

Ask your diamond to spin clockwise; this will realign all the light bodies with your higher self. It will stop when the alignment is complete. Stay with this healing for as long as feel to, allowing the ethereal colours to move through your system, attuning to your needs and soul requirements.

Feel the interwoven perfection between your physical body and crystalline matrix; they are now linked and communicating, feeding streams of consciousness into your mind, body and soul.

This diamond contains your perfected DNA and Light Code blueprints, allowing them to grow into activated life force throughout your beingness.

When you feel complete, give thanks for the sacred healing and to Mary and Jesus for their help. Drink lots of water and enjoy your day. Mary has also suggested making a spritz of orange blossom (neroli) and rose quartz to keep your light body uplifted. Do this when ever you feel the need for a top up or realignment.

Be aware your centre of gravity may shift slightly as you realign with your Soul Star, take it easy and enjoy the ride.

Summary of Light Codes 13-24

We are now opening our divine heart so that we open to our more divine aspects, our ancient memories of origin and who and what we are capable of. The codes of the compassionate heart and the connection of this compassion into our physical lives have occurred, allowing for a non-judgmental way of living. We now see the beauty all around us and forgive that which appears to be harmful and detrimental to creation. We are becoming even more embodied as our true soul-full selves, switched on and ready to step up into the new dimensions of existence and learning. As we move so we start to eliminate all that has stood in the way of our body/soul alignment and the upliftment into higher dimensional reality.

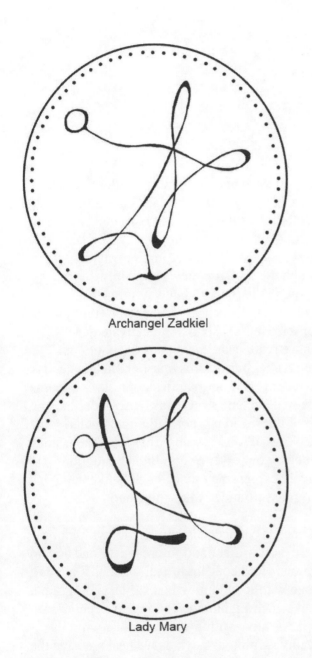

Chapter 10

Stellar Gateway Chakra

Light Codes 25-36

Archangel Jeremiel

The Stellar Gateway is situated about 15cm above the Soul Star. With this chakra we are entering Christ/Buddha consciousness and we are working as one in the unified fields of consciousness. We are now the One Heart; we have birthed into a much higher state of awareness and consciousness. When we are incarnating, our Soul Star moves through the Stellar Gateway and births us on earth. As we move through the Stellar Gateway we lose all our memories and our DNA Light Codes are deactivated (this was due to the fall into 3D consciousness). So as we reactivate these precious Light Codes we really start to connect back into our ancient source and remember our dreams, our light language, have access to the akashic records and our manifestation skills become even more acute. Life will become simpler as these codes become alive; we will be part of the world but not tied into its polarity of emotional confusion. We shall observe and truly see what is and how to navigate, guided by our essence into higher and more joyful ways of creatively expressing ourselves. It is like being in all worlds at once but fully grounded in the here and now.

This divine portal of energy connects us into the holographic universe. This is where past, present and future are all one and all events are occurring now. Hard concept to really get on a mental level, one just has to go with it and know it is so. The hologram is everything now just like each Light code/chakra has been discussed separately but is alive within every particle within us. All our past lives are alive within us now; as we heal we have the potential to delete these imprints from ourselves as well as from the earth's memory and holographic field. As we do this we are lightening the fields of light, from us, others involved, the earth and the universe as all things are in constant communication, reaction and action and so on. This is why there is so much deep cellular healing going on within us as we are healing on so many levels, within and around us as we are one with it all. So as we heal and en-light-en ourselves we cause an en-lightening holographically and we begin to ascend and the earth does also and the universe adjusts to enfold this new adjustment in its unified field of evolvement. En-lightenment is becoming lighter, more light and less weight of ego/karmic dust. Everything literally lightens and the truth can be seen and experienced, making life so much clearer and magical. Our collective grief shall heal and we will once again co create with each other to create a new and exciting future. We will learn to co- create with the creator to extend our potential to keep enlightening our selves into higher and greater states of enlightenment. From this state we explore and see just what can be achieved. It is an unknown future at this time as we are still discovering what we are capable of and what visions of excellence and beauty we can conceive of from our enlightened imaginations.

The Stellar Gateway is 6th dimensional energy, the Soul Star is 5th dimensional. This level of consciousness, once embraced, becomes part of who we are. It is not that we die and only operate as 6th dimensional spirit: this awareness integrates itself into our wholeness, becoming a level of consciousness we have access to and can embrace and develop the gifts that are available through this doorway. It is all very exciting and wondrous that we are moving into conscious awareness and embracing such divine states of being. Enlightened masters have these portals open and active which is why they are able to perform miracles and wonderful states of being. Many of these masters are able to bi-locate, that is, be in more than one place at a time, teleport themselves, heal others with a look as they see the all-ness of that being and can work through the hologram to heal on all levels the source of their ailment. Their conscious connection into the holographic universe enables them to instantly delete and heal. The list goes on and on of what can be achieved as we ascend our personal holographic spiral. It can be fascinating to learn about our past lives, they are a way to heal and to embrace lost gifts, to forgive and release trapped spirits caught into the astral fields of the hologram. We can also access curses and psychic intrusions that maybe infecting our light body and causing an illness or obstruction to our enlightenment. As we heal and strengthen these higher light codes we will find ourselves physically growing stronger as all these intrusions shall heal and dissolve out of our light body and codes. Do not get stuck with any of your memories, just acknowledge the lesson of it and let it go. Always make the intention that as you embrace the memory, pleasant or unpleasant, that it is now released and turned back into positive light and love energy. In this way we are continually clearing the hologram of light and lifting our vibration. Never let any unhappy vision of another hurting you hold you back by reigniting your pain, anger or other negative emotion as all you are doing is poisoning yourself, which is probably what was intended. Just intend forgiveness and let go knowing that with your intention the angels of grace and of love step in and create wholeness once again.

The Stellar Gateway will help you remember dreams and learn how to have lucid dreams. This can be quite useful when needing to understand situations or to receive guidance or inspiration. Do this by calling in and activating one's Stellar Gateway chakra before sleep. Ask for a message about a situation then await an answer in your dreams. This gateway will decode languages of light, symbols and information that is encoded into energy and colour, providing answers unavailable before this chakra was awakened. This gateway is a portal of manifestation also, so be careful what you day dream about.

The Stellar Gateway contains the silver ray energy. It is here that physical reality is birthed. So she is basically embracing quite a feminine energy. The rainbow rays are birthed here, the seven chakra colours, infrared for Earthstar and ultraviolet for the Soul Star. The next gateway will embrace the gold ray which is the masculine balance. Each of these rays is governed by a Lord of Light. The Lords of Light or ascended masters are apart of us also. Many sit on our own council of light that over sees the spiritual development of our spirit/soul. So doing the rituals and prayers assists us to connect with that master/ray/aspect of ourselves to heal and integrate on levels we may not have conscious access to. So because we are all apart of the same hologram they really are a divine part of who we are.

Light Codes 25-36

The information above really covers what these codes are all about, an embrace of our divine connection through our DNA into the hologram of existence. This causes an awakening and connection to our divine memories and gifts that can then activate and carry our physical experience into ever higher ways of being. We are becoming an embodiment of our divinity, living it and co creating with the one heart of consciousness. One's lunar light is awakened causing a divine feminine aspect of self to be born which gives us even greater access to manifesting our visions and goals. Our galactic councils of light become available to us through our inner awakening, thus we become our own master, connected to our council for divine guidance.

Archangel Jeremiel

AA Jeremiel is also known as Remiel. He is known as the angel of visions, dreams and seeing into the future. I feel he works well here as he operates from a timeless zone, where all time is now. I guess all the angels do but his area of expertise is time, presence and an understanding of the balance of actions. His vision allows us to see into the future, to access our soul's memories and heal imprints from past lives that no longer serve our higher good. In doing all this he is assisting us to reach our soul potential. Working through the Stellar Gateway he can help us access the akashic records and the Sacred Lores of the universe. I use the term Lore rather than Law as all our experiences throughout time have created our lore, our memories and learnings have created our law (lore) of balance. AA Jeremiel will bring messages in your dream state to assist you with life, helping you to remember them upon awakening. He will help us make our dreams/desires a reality, manifesting them into our lives. His knowledge is vast and made available to us through our workings with him. As we work with energy and healing, his streams of light work through us initiating the knowledge we need to heal and move forward in life.

Crystals to work with the Stellar Gateway

Lapis lazuli: Lapis helps us connect with ancient wisdom. Her silver/pyrite flecks connect beautifully with the silver ray. The deep indigo blue accesses the higher chakras and ancient vaults of knowledge, opening our third-eye so that we can "see" into these sacred places. There is a deep stillness in lapis that facilitates deep meditation, in this stillness we are able to access our memories and enter into sacred space with the masters and angels for healing and learning. Lapis is an ancient gift to us and she holds truth and wisdom for us from higher realms of teaching.

Celestite: beautiful celestial celestite, stone of light, love and angelic energy. She easily provides a doorway into higher realms and dimensions, uplifting one's vibration and connecting to a source of divine energy. The blue is a lovely ethereal, silvery shade, very feminine and perfect for this chakra. We can develop a sense of perfect trust, a slowing down and connection into that timeless place of spirit which is so healing and calming. Connecting to this timeless space greatly enhances the stellar state of being.

Angel Aura: the amazing ethereal colours in this crystal are so sublime and instantly lift your vibration into the celestial heavens. Any stone with the swirling ethereal colours is going to have a very high vibration. This crystal is clear quartz bonded with silver, platinum and other trace minerals, a perfect synergy to work with the stellar energies. She will work through the veils revealing past lives and future possibilities. Your guardian angel can connect to this crystal and bring you sweet dreams and loving support. Carry it on you when you need a little love and comfort, for she will clear the psychic pollution that often gathers and reveal an environment filled with peace and beauty.

Clear Quartz: clear quartz is always a great standby for she is able to embody and be programmed for all needs. She always reminds me of solid light, made available for us to carry, hold and work with at any time, she is such a blessing and easily available. There are many varieties of quartz: you will know when one calls you.

Moonstone: either the rainbow or the more milky version are great here as they are high vibration crystals that support the feminine energy to come into balance; assisting the intuition and the physical body to connect in an harmonious way, balancing hormones and helping them to upgrade their vitality, soothing the emotional body so that it feels comfortable to reawaken these ancient codes again.

Flower Essence for Stellar Gateway

Jasmine

Beautiful exquisite jasmine is a feminine moon energy flower perfect for our stellar essence. The scent of jasmine evokes the goddess energy and angelic light to blend with our energy, increasing our vibration and expanding our light body. This essence also contains Herkimer diamond and Lemurian record keeper crystals.

The essence works to:

Invoke higher divine love, silence and peace so our soul essence can merge more fully with our physical self

Accesses angelic music and communication which links us into our higher self and service

Clears our pranic tube of light which can be clogged with psychic pollution

Physically this works to clear mucus and mucus related diseases and lifts self-esteem

Accesses Akashic records for holographic healing of self and planet, clearing old karmic contracts

Connects new babies to their starry origins which help them settle into their new bodies.

Place a drop on belly button to reset your spiritual programs after a healing and on kidney points on the bottom of feet to ground in the spirit

Good meditation enhancer, lifts your vibration and strengthens the light body

Although a very feminine essence, jasmine assists to create balance between the inner male/female energy, thus assisting kundalini energy to rise and to balance one's inner polarity

Essential Oils to enhance Stellar Gateway

These chakras are very transpersonal, thus not having a very physical action but our essential oils can still assist us to maintain inner balance and harmony so that these fine and precious gateways can maintain their health and accessibility.

Jasmine: this oil will work to strengthen our divine female balance, bringing our spiritual essence into our sexual selves in a healthy and available way. She smells divine and makes a wonderful oil for anointing your chakras prior to meditation, or to create a sacred space for your love-making. Jasmine strengthens the sexual energy by bringing in a balance to one's inner male/female thus energising one's vitality. The heart energy is strengthened and inner joy is restored. Place a drop just below the naval to connect the spirit to one's creativity and sensual energy. They say that jasmine will draw angels into your light body to help you fulfil your dreams, if they are in alignment with your soul.

Melissa: Melissa comes to assist us to heal our programs around death, grief and loss. Loss is inevitable on the physical plane and to grieve is healthy but we also need to keep going and not allow the loss to reinforce our beliefs and fears around death. Melissa will help to ease the grief and keep you connected to your spirit and soul essence during the heavier times of grief. Place some on your crown chakra to create a space for spirit to support you through your process, this in turn helps the departed to also cross over with more ease and grace, our grief does not block them and our open spirit lights the pathway forward for them. A drop on the heart in times of grief will act like a cleansing breath of fresh air, lightening the heaviness and replacing it with love and understanding.

Immortelle: immortelle keeps our heart and spirit in balance, allowing the spiritual insights and messages to always come through in a compassionate way. This is so essential when doing spiritual work with others. She grounds us in divine love and assists us to live under the mantel of this love. As our psychic centres expand we want to make sure that what we perceive is received in a loving way, not in an analytical way which when shared is delivered in a rather uncompassionate way. Immortelle otherwise known as *helichrysum*, heals our separation from spirit, easing our awareness back into an integrated whole. When there is integration through the chakras, it allows for ancient knowledge within us to surface and assist us in our return to oneness. Immortelle also supports the liver, gall bladder, kidneys and pancreas to keep energised and healthy, great for upgrading your systems health in accord with your spiritual growth.

Rose Geranium: this oil is renowned for its wonderful healing properties in relationship to the balancing of the feminine energies. She will harmonise the hormones, giving them the support they need whatever stage of life you are in. Geranium is also good for healing the aura and repairing any holes and tears. This works wonderfully well with the Stellar Gateway as it paves the way for the integration of our divine feminine pathways, holographically healing the damage done to the divine feminine blueprint.

Ritual of Activation for the Stellar Gateway and Light Codes 25-36

A white or silver candle

Sage or frankincense to smudge and purify your space

Chosen oil for candle and self anointing

Stellar Gateway sigil … AA Jeremiel

Chosen crystal

Stellar Gateway essence, if available. (Remember you can invoke the essence into you by asking the deva of the essence to infuse your energy with her healing light.)

Smudge or infuse oils or incense to cleanse space

Say prayer of protection

Place candle in a safe container with sigil either drawn on candle or placed under candle holder

Anoint candle with oil

Hold your crystal or place nearby

Take your essence or invoke its energy into yourself. Play some soft meditative music and get into a nice and relaxed state, do some deep breathing to release any tension then bring your breath back to a gentle rhythm. Bring your focus inward and focus on what you are about to undertake, feel your heart softly open and receptive to your healing.

Invoke AA Jeremiel

"In the name of love and light I ask my guides, celestial helpers and AA Jeremiel to please open, activate and balance my Stellar Gateway chakra, placing within it the crystalline structures and sacred geometries I need to fully bring my Stellar Gateway chakra into its highest vibration and health activation. I ask that all the corresponding Light Codes, 25 through to 36 be brought into harmony with my soul's highest expression now. I command the activation of the 25th through to the 36th light codes now, bringing them into their highest level of presence on every level of my light body and through every chakra and bodily system now. I ask that all my light Codes come into harmony with each other, each supporting the harmonious action of the other as a unified whole. I am so grateful for this healing, thank you, Om Mani Padme Hum."

Relax and allow the guides, masters and angels to support you and provide healing as you activate your awakening. See pure white light flowing down through your higher chakras, building all the layers of your light body, bringing them into alignment with this new awakening. There may be a silvery tinge to the light; the silver is a very powerful healing energy that will work deeply through your cellular matrix to embed your true blueprint of wholeness. Relax, knowing that all has been put in motion. The angels and your connection to the universal wholeness will ensure a healing that will be for your highest good. Just keep relaxing and allowing your faith and belief in your own light and worthiness to build and become one with you. Sometimes it is good to know that the less you do the more can happen. This is one of those moments!

Animal Totem

The crane

Animal totems probably are not necessary here but the crane is so suitable. He stands so still, just being and feeling the breeze softly ruffle his feathers and knowing that when it is time to take action as there is food about, he will just know, because in his stillness all is already known to him. He does not stress about it, he just knows that he will know. He stands on one leg, like he is doing yoga, so perfectly balanced, barely observing his surroundings but when it is time to move he can strike swiftly or take flight in a most graceful and majestic way.

Mantra

This is a mantra from a different lineage but one I find very uplifting and healing. Chanting this mantra will put you in touch with the inner guru which in turn becomes the universal source of love and divine upliftment.

Guru Guru Wahe Guru

Guru Ram Das Guru

Chant this on awakening to connect into the divine and before falling asleep to uplift your vibration and invite healing as you sleep. Repeat as many times as feels comfortable. The mantra can uplift your energy beyond the day to day trials keeping us fresh and aligned with divine love and healing.

Goddess Work

Lady Nada

Lady Nada comes to us from the third ray of divine love and the seventh ray of violet light and the Aquarian age. She sits on the karmic board and is a bearer of light and hope as we move our lives forward and upward into a new age. Her twin flame is Sananda who is an aspect of Jesus Christ. Sananda and Lady Nada work closely together holding the energy of divine love and union for us as we heal and rebalance our own inner male and female energy. This rebalancing is all about creating unification in the polarities of not only ourselves but also the planet. Lady Nada was a high priestess in the temple of Divine Love during the times of Atlantis; her symbol is a soft pink rose which she offers us as a key to our own feminine healing. It is time to learn to love yourself unconditionally, to heal and release any programs that interfere with your own inner love and light from expanding into its highest potential. Her desire is to fill us with lofty thoughts, experiences of oneness, pure love and the magic of life in all her forms.

Lady Nada's first guidance for working with her is to continually bring yourself back into the vibration of joy. Joy is what lifts our vibration, assisting us to connect with 5th dimensional energy and work more closely with the angels and masters to co create a new and exciting reality. Joy will lift you above the heavier energies that often come into play in our lives, once you reconnect with a joyous thought denser energies are less able to affect you, protecting your health and general well being. It sounds simple but once again it takes vigilance to keep coming back to joy and not buying into those all too familiar woes that can drag you down into a lower vibrational field of life.

Quick fixes:

Close your eyes and remember a really happy time, allow that feeling to really fill you up, feel the happy energy and stay with it until you feel back on top of things.

Play some music that you love, music can shift energy so quickly. Move your body, feel the sounds all through out your physical and light body.

Walk in nature, the sheer beauty of our natural world leaves no room for feeling low.

Smell some flowers, sit next to a tree, go for a swim or paddle, listen to the birds singing or a creek gurgling ... all guaranteed to lift your energy.

Take a couple of deep breaths, silently or out loud chant your favourite mantra.

Be still, read a book, do something you love, eat something yummy.

Write down in a journal something to be grateful for every day, write down a list of your favourite joy activators so it is as easy as looking up an idea and going for it.

Many of us light workers have been through a lot to get where we are today; we were the ones who cut through the heavier earth karma so that the new day could dawn. The downside of that job is that sometimes we forget how to have fun, that it is now time to have fun, that the heavier work is done and now we have to learn that it is also about the joy of being alive. Lady Nada wishes so deeply to help us with this, to heal our hearts and lift our golden spirits back up, to show us who we really are, what amount of spiritual strength and light it took us as souls to do the work we have done. Do not get lost in the illusion of what has been. Be here now and see with eyes of light just what a miracle we have performed: it is not every day you get to evolve a planet in a few short years.

Ritual of Female Immortality Gene

This is a simple process that brings your sacred female codes back into alignment with your present day human expression. This is also appropriate for men as we all have a male/female side. You can do this process as often as you feel the need, we are all continually evolving and by doing these rituals regularly you assist the alignments to grow stronger and anchor in your ever-shifting light fields.

The ritual is about activating your pure feminine blueprint. Much healing of old karmic imprints and damage has been achieved. Now it is time to activate our healing codes, to resurrect our own divine imprint that was put in place eons ago, before we fell and lost our memories. Doing this ritual will start a process that will unfold an inner healing that will support your system to rejuvenate more easily, from the inside out. It starts a process that brings together all the activations that we have been doing throughout this book. There is a unification of the light codes, another layer of bringing them into a greater whole so that they can truly start to sing your true vibration and essence again. This is a sacred alchemy of life, true life that is working a magic inside of you to awaken dormant codes of lives lived for much longer than we are used to. You already have this information within you; the processes are simply reactivating them. Sometimes colds, flu or other discomforts can occur as your body sloughs off the old so that the new can resurface. Take care of yourself, drink plenty of water, teas and juices, make this a time to pamper and take care of yourself.

Create your sacred space

Light a candle and anoint with chosen oil

Place the Lady Nada, Isis and Sananda sigils on your body: Nada over your heart, Isis over your navel and Sananda on your brow.

Anoint your heart, third eye and navel chakras with some rose, neroli, frankincense or lavender essential oil.

Drink some water infused with the energy of moonstone and Herkimer diamond or clear quartz.

Say:

"Beloved Lady Nada and the Ladies of Shambhala, please infuse me with joy and sacred laughter, that I may raise my vibration into attunement with my higher self and feminine truth.

I ask for a healing of my ancient immortal feminine blueprint, that my cellular memory be reactivated to its highest level of health and rejuvenation.

Fill the space within me with happiness and wonder, joy and vital life force, reuniting me with my truth and highest vision of self.

I ask for the deletion of past and limiting belief systems, of curses and all negative interference, that I may return to my inner Shambhala, refilled with her light and beauty, connected to my soul's truth and wisdom forever more.

Please fill my heart with eternal light, revivifying my immortal presence and love that I may forever more know who I am in truth and knowledge.

Thank you, Om Mani Padme Hum."

Once you have said your prayer and laid out your body with the sacred objects, allow yourself some time to meditate, visualising a yin yang symbol over your pelvic region.

It is silver and white with black markings delineating the image, dividing the silver side from the white.

The holy beings of light, including Lady Nada, gather around you, their energy a gentle and soothing presence.

Ask silently for the yin yang symbol to spin clockwise.

It starts off spinning slowly but as its light does its work the spin increases in speed, going deeper into your cells and out into your light body.

Say:

"I call down the Silver Ray to cleanse and purify my physical and light body of all potential disease and darkness. Please process and purify my system on all levels, leaving me sparkling with healing effervescing light now, thank you."

The spin lifts the old crystallised debris from your cells; it simply lifts the old and dissolves it back into the light. The energy of the symbol is accessing your timeline through your hologram, dissolving, in all time and space, old implants and imprints of interference to your divinity.

Be still and rest, trusting and allowing this healing to occur. All things happen in their own time, organically and safely so there is nothing to fear, only a lightening and freeing up of your health and well being. It is important to realise you are always in control of what feels right for you and just how much shifting you can deal with in any given ritual and time frame. The universe works to help you at your speed of evolution and what your body can handle and how far you would wish to go with any programs that are occurring to evolve us. Release with love and know you are being divinely guided through these times, be at peace for all is well.

Activities that assist your body to assimilate the energy:

Yoga and breathing exercises

Drinking pure water and using vibrational essences

Walking in nature

Chanting the mantras

Avoiding old situations/people that compromise your healing experience.

Summary of Light Codes 25-36

The Stellar Gateway and corresponding codes offer us a doorway to access these ancient memories from the akasha and ancient mysteries. The Gateway accesses the hologram thus feeding through directly into our Light Codes and switching them back on. We can access our true divinity through these higher gateways. By bringing it all together in this way we are reactivating our star gates and ancient galactic knowledge and then embodying and rebirthing it back into our physical selves, thus ascending whilst still being in a physical body. By doing it this way we are also ascending our beloved Gaia, raising her vibrational field so that we all grow as one. New doorways of magic and elemental awareness shall show us the way. As we take a step, so too does Gaia, expanding our potentials and implementing heaven on earth.

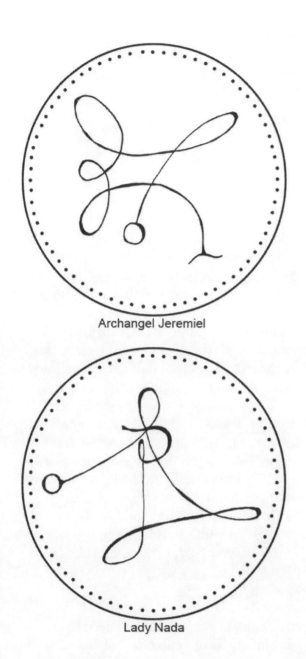

Chapter 11

Universal Gateway Chakra

Light Codes 37-48

Archangel Uriel

The Universal Gateway is found approximately 15cm above the Stellar Gateway. This gateway merges us into 7th dimensional energies. We become one with the creator and prepare to move our consciousness into the infinite. This gateway allows us to embody this infinite awareness whilst still being in a body: this then connects us into the infinite flow of universal consciousness. As this happens we are as one with the creator, living our life as one with divine creation, knowing and being in oneness in all our activities. I believe this state of being is possible whilst still being a physically alive human being. Maybe also we are closer to this state of being than we realise. Once we heal our ego self and stop the endless merry go round of karmic healing it will probably be revealed that it was this state of consciousness that guided us back into alignment with our truth - it was unconsciously active all along. These higher centres are getting stronger as we heal. It is their awakening presence and ancient preset programming that is guiding our evolvement and spiritual healing. The light we receive from these gateways carries us through some deep cellular healing, providing miracles and healing that would defy the medical system. They provide us with a powerful spiritual life force that guides us. It is like a forcefield that supports us as we break down, like a cocoon surrounding a chrysalis. We are the butterfly that eventually emerges.

Our cocoon of light provides all the knowledge we need to get where we are going, it is directly linked into our soul and all the power we have accumulated throughout our many lifetimes. The knowledge flows through our light body, fed from our soul through our gateways. Our DNA then receives the information and creates our divine expression. When too much karmic influence is lodged in our unconscious mind it then interferes with our divine connection and so we buy into the fears and other programs that seem very real. In learning to be still we can access our vital soul information through the gateway and infuse it in to our physical lives. We learn to flow in the light stream of love that connects us to our universal self and so become our true expression of self. Surrendering to this light flow need not be difficult. Just let all the worries go, hand them over to the divine and let go, take a breath and learn to flow. You will know all you need to know when you need to know it. This flow, and becoming receptive to it, is once again reintegrating the divine receptivity of the inner goddess. She receives all she needs through her magnetic love frequency; it all comes back to self love.

Where the Stellar Gateway is lunar, the Universal Gateway is solar. The lunar is the silver ray and the solar comes in on the gold ray. The gold ray is the vibration that holds the wisdom of the divine that permeates all of creation. These are like the divine laws of the universe and creation. The gold and silver rays are the divine male and female energies, the beginning point where we began to split off from our oneness and become polarised. They contain all we need to harmonise our balance and reunite with wholeness, to integrate the knowledge and unify our kundalini again, thus create ascension within and without. The silver ray, being feminine, births the solar knowledge into form. The Universal Gateway is strongly linked to the solar plexus chakra as it is about grounding divine will, so the golden light of the solar plexus assists with the anchoring and activating of the divine gold solar energy, putting into action heaven on earth and divine law and knowledge, expressed through the development of one's divine will. The gold ray is like pure sunshine, a burning brightness that defies our ability to look into for the sheer magnitude of its brilliance. This bright wonder is pure life force and intelligence; it takes us into a deep healing in order to purify us to the point where we can become this light, to allow its bright burn to purify our energy centres so that we can consciously begin to operate within this spectrum. This does not mean we walk around looking blindingly bright but that we have released enough of the unconscious mind junk to become this beacon of spiritual truth and to embody the state of awareness and enlightenment this can bring. This is desirable but be patient and enjoy the journey. Just know that if you are reading this then you have set this course in motion. Whether it happens this year, this lifetime or in five life times it does not matter as you are already starting to embody this amazing source of energy and brilliance into your life. The masters and angels who watch over us and our universe will be with you assisting this new state of awareness to keep expanding within you. They know the exact speed and capacity you have to do this without it burning you out. To go too fast will burn you out and cause a nervous system break down. This usually only happens with the use of psychotropic drugs or an over zealous approach to sacred kundalini practices.

Light Codes 37-48

One is really starting to become and awaken one's multidimensionality. This state of being is awakening throughout the DNA and thus connecting one's wholeness into this level of awareness and knowledge. There is alchemy in these codes for they bring the unification of lunar/solar energy, so in effect your inner polarity is merging and becoming balanced. No more mood swings? Let's hope so. The language of light is becoming stronger; healers will transfer not only healing energy but the knowledge will be encoded into the healing energy, assisting the entity to heal themselves. Telepathy is also a language of light, only accessed once our judgement has healed and unification of self has occurred. "Light bulb" moments occur more frequently as your light body is able to access all the information you need. Life just flows, as all is directly sourced from universal consciousness. As these codes activate and grow strong you will be able to source all the gifts that you have developed over your many lifetimes, bringing them into the now. Even future gifts may start to manifest. Who knows what the quantum fields of potential have in store for us. No one knows how this will unfold as it is a pure act of creation unfolding within us now. We may access new and amazing healing technologies, light codes of language yet unknown, symbols that will unlock ancient, yet future, technologies that will help us create an eco friendly world. Let's go a little further ... wormholes in space and time that we will navigate with our consciousness and access unknowable and divine understandings. We may not have to eat as much in order to nourish. Our bodies will be able to nourish on less as we shall be able to extract the energy and light from the food and easily absorb this into our body. This type of existence is very Lemurian, our light bodies shall be connected and switched on in the divine matrix of light, and drawing all we need effortlessly into existence as what we want will automatically be of benefit to all. As we have all plugged into this state of being, it means that what we create is in flow with the divine directive of all that is, so all we are benefits as one in our co-creation of beauty and creative excellence. What the individual perceives of as lovely will add dimension and beauty to the whole, the environment and the individual, each bringing something unique and wonder-full.

Archangel Uriel

Uriel's name means Light of God or Fire of God. The Universal Gateway is all about the solar light of God. Uriel watches over the Universal laws; he helps us to find solutions to our earthly issues and assists us to make our earthly lives as abundant as possible. He is like an oracle, always ready to help us understand and implement new ideas and visions. He gives us those 'Ah Haa' moments that illuminate our pathway. AA Uriel helps us to create heaven on earth, assisting us to see and implement new and creative ways of manifesting. He is our divine companion who knows all that we are through out all time and space and is here to help us become all that we can be. His knowing of us so intimately allows for him to assist us on every level to become our own beacons of light, reweaving our soul's journey back into wholeness so that we can draw upon our true potential to heal us and mobilise us towards our oneness and creative splendour. My sense is that he is a being of vast intelligence. His intelligence assists the workings of creation to unfold with order and balance.

Universal Gateway Crystals

Citrine: the golden yellow hues of citrine are perfect for linking into the Universal Gateway. Citrine is a wonderful manifestation crystal; she is clear, pure and vibrant, full of light and clarity. Using citrine shall also link the solar plexus with the Solar Gateway assisting in the anchoring of this magnificent light, working it into the light body, strengthening the connection and uplifting oneself into these supernal planes of consciousness. Used with intention, citrine makes an invaluable ally for working with these higher chakras and gateways, building the strength of the solar plexus to enable it to handle the high frequencies transmitted from the Universal Gateway. Citrine will build the will, cleansing the solar plexus of old outdated emotional and mental programs and gradually anchor in the updated frequencies that are transmitting from your higher gateways.

Clear Calcite: clear calcite comes in a rhombohedral shape (like a cube). It is clear and assists in seeing things in a multifaceted way. She will greatly help in connecting to the manifestation energy available through the higher gateways, allowing for a multidimensional view of things. The calcite will also illuminate what may be hindering the manifestation, like what is jamming up the process and interfering with the flow. She will assist in clearing these road blockages thus opening up awareness beyond the ordinary. The third eye is stimulated which helps one to perceive the higher perspectives and to thus see and feel more clearly what one is achieving. This gives more energy to the manifestation process.

Ruby: ruby carries ancient codes and memories. Being red she holds a lot of energy and is able to deeply access our physical self and awaken these ancient codes within our cells. Ruby also works very well with AA Uriel and assists with grounding his energy and adding a potent touch to our manifestation work. AA Uriel is a wonderful angel to call on for help with this, his immense power really drives home our dreams and desires. He adds fuel to the fire of our deepest desires and beautiful ruby enhances this energy.

Star rubies are particularly good for this and rubies in general empower our kundalini thus energizing our own emanations of power and creativity.

Moldavite: moldavite is said to be part of a meteorite. Whether it was created from the impact of the meteor onto the earth or is a piece of broken off meteor is still in debate but how ever it was formed it is a very high frequency stone and well suited to working with the higher chakras. Moldavite being green in colour helps to raise our heart energy, opening it to receive much needed knowledge and healing. This in turn helps our nervous system download this knowledge, upgrading our systems to clear the earth plane and connect with our galactic heritage. Because of its high frequency, moldavite offers a powerful spiritual protection. Negative energies are unable to penetrate the field of light that Moldavite offers: this then assists with our connection to our guides and higher sources of knowledge. Moldavite can catalyse deep shifts in one's life, she will work on what needs healing in your light body and chakras, connect one with guides, boost spiritual vitality and speed spiritual development. All this aligns well with connecting and working with the Universal Gateway and AA Uriel.

Flower Essence for the Universal Gateway

Gardenia

The gardenia is such a beautiful flower, she draws angel light into her scent and soft petals. Her energy connects us with such heavenly forces and angelic realms. An angelic energy that connected with me during the making of this essence was Seraphina, an angel who is part of the Seraphim, one of the highest dominions of angelic orders. Taking the essence leaves your light body feeling pearlescent and glowing with other worldly light. When making your own essence, remember to add clear quartz or Herkimer diamond to the water as they will amplify the energy.

Works to activate and balance the Universal Gateway and connect us to it in our light bodies.

Heals the connection through the matrix of light. This then enables you to download your sacred codes of light and live in a state of bliss, feeling connected to the divine in a grounded way.

Opens the heart up to divine healing and guidance.

Increases psychic awareness, spiritual guidance, clairaudience and prophesy skills.

Opens doors to soul retrieval work, DNA healing and enhances meditation.

Sprinkle drops in your baby's bath, cleanses their energy and makes them smile.

Scented Rosemary, Elestial Quartz, Ruby … Lord Sananda's Essence.

I was given this blend to create an essence that would resonate with Lord Sananda, who is the oversoul of Jesus. It feels appropriate to work with it here as we had Lady Nada who is his twin soul in the lunar gateway and we shall marry the Solar and Lunar Gateways together within us through the divine connection of these two.

Instant access to healing and clearing of energy body.

Clarifies the mind, unlocking it to find answers and guidance.

Opens the heart to love allowing one to see situations through the eyes of compassion. Makes a connection to the masters, angels and guides.

Provides protection, creates a shimmering current of light that repels darkness, use as a personal protection and as a mist for sick rooms and general home protection. Works well this way when you invoke AA Uriel, Gabriel, Michael and Raphael.

Message from Sananda:

"This essence tends the sick, it awakens one's own ability to self heal. It protects and creates a connection to one's higher self for truth and courage, conviction and love, helping one to carry forth one's mission in life. This essence is designed to keep you connected to and opened up to your Christed self, strengthening and growing one's Christed light body, guiding one into service and the Light."

This essence is like a spiritual emergency essence. Place directly on any chakra for deep physical, emotional and spiritual healing. Use with other essences to enhance their healing effects. Will assist in accessing one's healing codes for self repair.

Magnolia with Jade, Labradorite and Kunzite ... Quan Yin

This is the energy signature I was given for working with Quan Yin energy, to access her frequency and healing gifts. Her energy is incredibly full of grace and mercy but also strength and centeredness. This is her gift to us, to be able to hold these frequencies whatever we are doing. She is very psychic and offers us tools to help us carry this gift without it undoing us.

Increases spiritual perception, opening psychic centres and connecting them to a divine frequency.

Unblocks old wounds, offering them back to the light for healing.

Dissolves old karmic contracts that are no longer valid but are still affecting your well being. Just being aware that an issue needs addressing and taking the drops will dissolve and clear the issue. Not everything we are healing needs to be fully understood. Often it is an inherited condition that we agreed to heal, it is not necessarily our personal learning curve.

Creates clarity and centeredness in an easy and organic way allowing you to feel steady through change.

Great for mediums as it initiates contact and shielding all at once.

Clears old family contracts and frees your genetic codes to be healed and reprogrammed.

Spray it around people who are passing away to clear old thought forms that may hinder their passing; works like a spiritual disinfectant.v

Assists councillors and healers who hold a lot of energy for others, it provides a centering and grounding, a connection to higher frequencies to keep your energy up.

Essential oils to enhance the Universal Gateway healing and connection

At this point the chakra and Light Code energy is so high that there would not be one oil that was quite so high but they can help us to physically prepare to embody these higher frequencies.

Neroli is always an uplifting and angelic scent. She will attune your energy to the higher frequencies of light, soothing your nervous system and opening your crown chakra to embrace these changes and upliftment. Neroli instils trust that then allows us to feel safe enough to once again open ourselves up to the heavenly light body. Self defeating attitudes will melt away, feelings of not being good enough or worthy enough to become one with your higher self. She reunites heart and soul, self love can then take hold, opening the inner doorways to the infinite.

Ginger: wonderful, spicy, warm ginger will strengthen the physical body, stimulating the endocrine system, enhancing sexual energy and physical vitality. All these are vitally important for us if we are to successfully ground these higher frequencies and not be burnt up by their Light. Ginger will stimulate etheric enzymes, allowing for new realities to be easily digested and assimilated. She will literally warm your system, physical and spiritual, drawing towards you what you need for your growth; growth that is guiding you towards embracing more of your higher truth and expression. By stimulating the sexual organs one's creativity gets a boost so that new and amazing ideas can be birthed in a grounded way. Ginger stimulates the etheric body if used in massage oil which replenishes the physical as well. She will move blocked emotional energy, making way for transpersonal experiences to occur clearly and more often. A vital and healthy physical body definitely enhances the spiritual birthing and ascension process. Ginger can also awaken memories of Lemurian lifetimes, enabling the reconnection of ancient gifts.

Frankincense awakens spiritual and soul purposes. This oil is able to reach into the higher frequencies of light effortlessly and holds much healing and wisdom. Frankincense is a cell regenerator so is marvellous used in massage blends, anointing chakras or in a spray bottle, as the oil will assist with the healing that occurs as we peel back the old memories and renew ourselves. She will assist us to recover our soul's blueprint thus implementing deep healing on every level. Frankincense oxygenates the body. As this oxygenation process takes hold it expands our spiritual abilities and new realities can be perceived. This is truly a God Essence as far as essential oils go. It is more a male energy oil and is ruled by the sun which makes it perfect solar oil.

Ritual of Activation for the Universal Gateway and Light Codes 37-48

A white, gold or lemon coloured candle

Frankincense or sage to smudge and cleanse space

Chosen oil for anointing and candle dressing

AA Uriel sigil

Chosen crystal

Universal essence for spraying above your crown and/or taking

Smudge and cleanse your space with either frankincense incense or sage smudge

Say prayer of protection

Place candle in a fire proof container and either draw the sigil on it or place it underneath

Anoint candle with oil

Hold your crystal or place it on your heart or on altar with candle

Take your essence and place some on the crown of your head (this way it directly accesses the pineal and pituitary energy vortex and enhances the integration of the vibration)

Place yourself in a relaxed position, play soft meditation music if you wish, take some deep breaths, bringing yourself into a very relaxed and open state. Feel each muscle unwinding as each breath takes you deeper and deeper into a meditative and receptive state.

Invoke AA Uriel

"In the name of love and light I ask my guides, celestial helpers and Archangel Uriel to please open, activate and balance my Universal Gateway chakra, placing within it the crystalline structures and sacred geometries I need to fully bring the Universal Gateway chakra into its highest vibration and health activation. I ask that all the corresponding Light Codes, 37 through to 48 be brought into harmony with my soul's highest expression now. I command the activation of the 37th through to the 48th Light Codes now, bringing them into their highest level of presence on every level of my light body and beingness. I ask that all my Light Codes come into harmony with each other, each

supporting the harmonious action of the other as a unified whole. I AM so grateful for this healing thank you. OM Mani Padme Hum."

Relax and allow the guides, angels and masters who work with you and this healing to do their work. Keep going deeper and deeper. The deeper you go the clearer your channels and connections to these sacred, high vibrational fields of light become. Once this opening begins amazing downloads of light and knowledge can occur, no effort, no strain, just effortless grace cascading down upon and within you. The guides, your higher self and masters all watch over you, monitoring how much you are ready and able to integrate. Within the silence everything can be accessed, the more familiar you become with this state of organic peace, self acceptance and inner stillness, the more accessing these sacred truths will become second nature, once again you will know what you need to know when you need to know it. Surrender and trust that you are a child of the universe doing an amazing task. Allow our friends of the light to carry you for awhile, let go and just be.

Animal Totem

Praying mantis

Imagine the stillness of the praying mantis. He holds so still, silently allowing life to provide for him, his silent prayer always answered for he knows his connection to the web of life. He does not doubt the point of his existence he just silently moves and sways to the inner and outer rhythms of life. All his senses are awake and aware, he has no inner noise to interfere with his transmissions of knowing. In his silence he knows all that he needs to know and so moves within that silence knowing all is provided and his experience just *is*. Imagine the relief of letting it all go and becoming a human being instead of a human doing and doing and doing…

He truly is the guru you have always been looking for!

Mantra

Chinnamasta is an Indian goddess called upon for raising kundalini to the top most spiritual centre and creating a state of "no mind". She will assist in surrendering the ego control leading to service of the enlightened mind. Her energy carries you beyond your comfort zones, stretching the essence to embrace more truth and less ego control. Are you ready to become psychologically naked? Ha, I love it!

"Aum shrim hrim aim vajra-vairochneeyai hum hum phat svaha"

(Ohm Shreem hreem ai-eem vaj-ra-vai-ro-cha-nee-ai hoom hoom fuht swuh-huh)

Shrim stands for beauty; hrim for transformation and creativity.

Vajra-vairochaneeyai is the name of Chinnamasta that means "thunderbolt lightning of spiritual awakening".

Hum is a mantra for cutting through all illusions.

Phat focuses the power in the mantra.

Swaha means "offering to the fire of consciousness".

Her consort is Shiva. As you can imagine this is a powerful coupling, driving the enlightened mind through all illusions, opening the chakras and activating the cosmic dance of love.

Goddess Work

We will primarily work with Kuan Yin but I would also like to do a brief ritual to unite the energy of Lady Nada (our lunar goddess) and Lord Sananda (the solar companion). When we unite their essence within us we open ourselves to a divine blueprint of spiritual union and wholeness. As they are both ascended masters, they provide us with a very enlightening way to unite our solar and lunar aspects in the higher realms and then download them into our physical existence. This was part of what their experience was for, to cut a pathway for us to follow, to reunite our polar opposites and reunite our wholeness, through divine love and holy union from within.

Invocation of the Gold Ray

"I now call upon the ray of golden solar light to infuse my system with pure potential and illumination. I ask the golden ray to empower and strengthen my divine force on all levels, guiding me home to my true and illuminated higher self, Om Mani Padme Hum."

The Silver ray is included here for the balancing effect.

"I now call upon the silver ray of lunar light to prepare me on every level to purify, heal and embody my full goddess potential, Om Mani Padme Hum".

Lunar and Solar Unification Ritual

One white or silver candle

A yellow crayon or yellow candle

Frankincense and rose or rose geranium essential oils, mixed and diluted in a little carrier oil

Lord Sananda's and Lady Nada's sigils

A rose quartz and a ruby, garnet or citrine crystal

Two clear quartz crystals

A special bowl filled with spring water, some drops of the essential oils mentioned above and the crystals placed within it also (not the clear quartz).

Say the prayer of protection

Place bowl of spring water on altar

On the right side place Sananda's sigil and on the left place Lady Nada's sigil, then place one clear quartz crystal on each sigil.

Hold the white or silver candle and very carefully melt some of the yellow crayon wax over the white candle until you have some drips running down the sides. This is for merging the golden light of the solar energy into the silver/white light of the lunar energy. Then place this in front of your bowl of spring water.

Anoint yourself with some of the special oil you have created, put some on your brow, heart, solar plexus and sacral chakras.

Say:

"I call upon the divine and holy energies of Lady Nada and Lord Sananda. Please assist me in uniting my inner solar and lunar energy, creating a magical union of wholeness and sublime love. I ask to enter the inner temple of holy oneness with myself and all that I AM, forever more united in holy matrimony with my inner divinity. May my union be a beacon of light for others to become awakened and whole within themselves. I give thanks to Lady Nada and Lord Sananda for the gift of your blessed love and the pathway of divine union you have carved for us all to follow in. Om Mani Padme Hum."

Lie down and make yourself comfortable. See the infinity symbol above your head: it is moving and swirling with silver and gold light. It starts to spin even faster and streams of silver and gold light start to flow from the united centre of the symbol, flowing in through your crown chakra. As they flow down they begin to wind around themselves, entwining together like two snakes. This movement of the two streams of silver and gold light continues to flow down your spine, each vertebrae being one twist in the spiral; they wrap themselves around your spine, forming a perfect spiral from your crown to the base of your spine. See that they are still moving and pulsing with light; as they spiral they are drawing the yin yang energies of your essence into a harmonious whole. The movement and energy the spiral creates is transforming any old outdated programs, wounds and imprints from your cellular makeup, leaving you a clear vessel to embody this new union and healing. The spiralling is moving up and down at the same time, dancing to its own rhythm as it courses its way through your energy matrix and recalibrates your personal balance.

Stay in this space as long as you feel to. When you are complete, take the water from your bowl and use it in a bath, as a hair rinse, foot bath, spritzer or however you feel to. The water contains the blending of your solar and lunar energies and is a lovely way to complete and integrate on a physical level the healing that took place.

As an extra you could write out a love wish list, naming some qualities you would like in a partner, even in a present relationship to assist you in creating the right love connection that will unify and uplift your essence. Place the paper under the candle when you do the ritual, this will empower the working even more, bringing the right situation to compliment your inner balance.

Kuan Yin

Kuan Yin is often called the female Buddha; she is a being of divine mercy, compassion and protection. It is said that she will answer every prayer sent her way. Kuan Yin is not only an ascended master and goddess she is also a Bodhisattva, which means an enlightened being. When Kuan Yin had the opportunity to become a Buddha she chose to stay within reach of human hearts so that she could assist in the enlightenment of all beings, she felt their pain and chose to help release us from the bondage of this limited consciousness. Just by saying her name you will feel a deep peace, a gentleness that will bring you into a state of calm and no mind. Her name instils a protection also, this goddess is a mighty being and her strength is powerful ... gentle as she is.

A mantra to invoke Kuan Yin

"Namo Kuan Shi Yin Pu Sa"

(Nah-moh Kwahn Shee Yin Poo Sah)

"Salutations to the most compassionate and merciful Bodhisattva Kuan Yin"

When needing to connect to Kuan Yin's most benevolent, loving and wise energy, simply light a candle and chant her mantra, chant it nine times to establish a link.

You may wish to tell her of your personal issues. If so, prepare a bowl of water infused with flowers, sea salt, essential oils and/or essences. As you share your feelings allow the water to absorb the emotions. When you have finished pour the water into the garden.

Anoint your chakras with an essential oil or flower/crystal essence and open your heart to her very special energy.

Light some incense. *Nag Champa* is always a great choice and easily found.

Simply by calling on her or using her mantra you will feel an instant peace. This mantra is well worth the effort of memorising.

For the home altar: Find a nice largish white candle, draw her sigil and mantra on the candle and anoint it with a favourite essential oil. Light it briefly each morning or evening, chant her mantra nine times to infuse your life and home with her blessings. Put the candle out after each blessing, that way it lasts a long time and continually carries the prayer. When the altar candle is nearly finished, light a new candle from the old one to continue the energy.

A great way to physically work with the integration of the solar/lunar balance is to do the alternate nostril yoga breath. Hold one nostril closed as you breathe in through the open one, hold then release breath through the other nostril. Take a breath in through this nostril, hold both shut then open first nostril and release the breath. Repeat as many times as you feel comfortable; this is a wonderful healing process to do, very balancing and soothing.

Summary of Light Codes 37-48

As these Light Codes activate they cause a new level of unification within your system. This may cause some ripples as this new level of male/female balance sorts itself out into a much higher level of union. The good news is that you shall feel so much clearer and your existing relationship should reach a new level, or it may end as it no longer has anything to teach you, or if you are single, the partner of your dreams just may finally arrive. This new level of peace and equilibrium shall allow your consciousness to reach new levels of awareness and understanding. The universe will start to open its doors wider and new opportunities to share your new expansion should occur. There will be new wisdoms and insights, less struggle and chaos. The chaos may still be going on but you shall feel too blissful to care. This inner union is a reflection of a union with oneness and the unified field of light that we are a part of. Information from the creative source is immediately received as you have unified with this source, so all you do you do as one with the divine. This signals the end of separation.

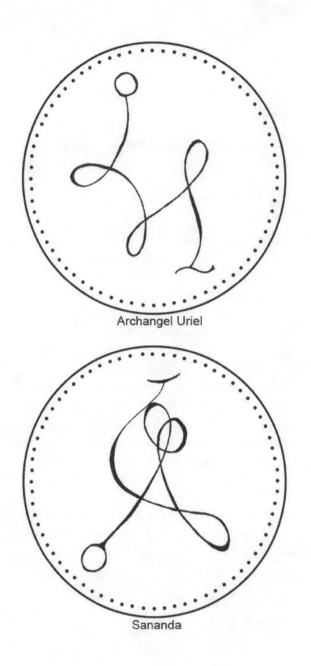

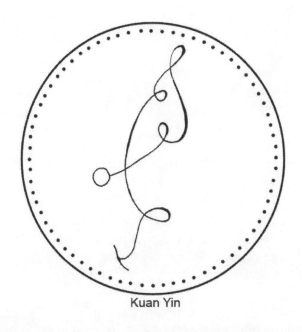
Kuan Yin

Chapter 12

Cosmic Gateway Chakra

Light Codes 49-64

Archangel Metatron

The Cosmic Gateway is situated in the Divine Plane, 15cm above the Universal Gateway. Through this gateway we become open to the limitless of all there is. This is also called the Void. All that is, unlimited peace is all that lives here, a total expansion and contraction of consciousness in the stillness, a unification of the sun, central sun and greater central sun, a unity of the Goddess/God self, creator and weaver of life.

The Cosmic Gateway has a mirror reflection in the Earth's Gateway. When we ground our energy into the heart of Mother Earth we are not only grounding ourselves but in effect also activating our Cosmic Gateway. This creates a vast alignment of our earthly/heavenly bodies … as above, so below. These two gateways create the zero fields of life and manifestation, back to zero point. The core earth energy rises and anchors in your Earth Star chakra. The geometry of the Cosmic Gateway is a twelve pointed star that contains all the rays, elements, sounds and directions to obtain wholeness and balance on every level in all space and time. This star is an acknowledgment of Metatron's Cube. It is an acknowledgment of the Wholeness of Creation contained through the Cosmic Gateway in all directions of time and space.

Within the star is contained all the elements, earth, air, fire and water, coming together at the central core which is the Zero Point Field or the field that connects all of creation. Through this zero point field the silver and gold rays are birthed, beginning the dance of creation and incarnation. Each of the twelve points represents the 12 dimensions, the centre being the 13th or zero point. On our journey of evolvement, we go through lifetimes where we embrace each one of these initiations in order to actualise our ascension and full human experience. For example, we may go through a series of deeply emotional lifetimes in order to bring balance to the Water Element. The Fire element may be about mastering your will. Air could be about harnessing the power of the mind to use for good and the Earth element could be about physical health and manifestation. As all these elements and rays come into balance we truly become the magician and mystic, able to manifest and become the ascended human being leading to new areas of growth and expansion. As we all zero in on this new sense of balance we shall shift our reality into a new and hopefully more enlightened experience. This coming together of your entire colour spectrum is like a switch turning on. As this happens, a new master is born, all the lifetimes become one experience and you are still an individual but are also inexplicably connected as one.

To truly activate and reconnect this chakra we have to have cleared and balanced our light and dark selves. All 'karma' has been balanced, our inner child is happy and free and we feel at peace with who we are. Because this chakra has such a large balance, remember as high as it is, it is also that deep. So all one's perceived darkness has to have come to light and been liberated from the dark unconscious part of the mind. As we meditate and do our activations and other inner growth exercises, we unwind this hidden core in our unconscious, releasing all our past programming and pain which allows our DNA to spiral back into a new and expanded state of presence. The core of our unconscious is alive in every particle of our DNA; remember all our seemingly separate parts are actually segmented parts of one whole, a whole that we are reuniting. As each of our chakras and Light Codes are rebalanced and healed we reweave the very fabric of our essence, opening the sacred doorway of supreme conscious awareness and soul reconnection. It is an alchemical reaction, like we finally find the correct code to "open sesame" the inner safe of our essence. It organically just opens like a flower in the sun, no effort or trying. In this way we are protected from opening too fast. As the unconscious unwinds, it allows an oxygenation and a space for more light to enter the cells, all systems working as one, no longer separated by the inner programs of separation and past emotional programming. This unwinding is also working on a vast level, for as we unwind we are unwinding the more negative 3D hold on the earth. As we release our past lives and heavy energy blocks we release the Earth from these same holds, as above so below, as we do the work, the Earth also follows.

To become our Buddha selves we must have forgiven ourselves completely, which believe it or not, is harder than forgiving others. Ponder this: you are a part of the Godhead, you chose to descend into physical form, you then chose lives that would allow you to experience leadership, royalty and other amazing feats of excellence but you also chose to experience darkness, of being the villain and corrupt bad guy just so that you could learn from it and then forgive it. How silly, but there we have it. This is how we truly learn compassion, by loving the whole of us … the good, the bad and the ugly. We all want to look good and see past lives of fame but how about those amazing dark moments. Learn to love and embrace everything. This does not mean it's ok to murder someone so you can forgive yourself, that is done and dusted. No, now we just clean up and we do this with forgiveness. There will be many who cross your path exhibiting bad or annoying behaviour. Forgive them: this is an opportunity to embrace more of yourself, to help reunify on many levels. This does not mean that you continue to be abused by them. Compassion allows for deep healing but with the advantage of detachment. As we learn to detach from life's drama we stop the karmic wheel of rebirth and pain, the zero point of consciousness is reached and all becomes one. We enter a state of equanimity of consciousness, stillness and peaceful acceptance, receptive grace and a totality of being.

Light Codes 49-64

These Light Codes are where the rainbow mist of wholeness becomes actualised in every cell of your body. This is your Godhead code; it holds the key to bringing your vibration to its highest level of your immortal soul's purpose. This key will activate all your Light Codes to their highest level of attunement, effectively creating heaven on earth, within and without. We are now once again in a unified state of wholeness with all of creation; we are fully connected as one in our consciousness, in every cell to everything. There is continual communication between us and the creator, our soul acts as one with the divine directives we receive, organically we are now in every cell connected to and as one with the Godhead. The spiritual energy of this gateway is like the mist of a rainbow. You cannot touch it but it is such a reflection of beauty, like the angelic waves of light showing us the magic of other dimensional realities through its prisms of colour and light. You cannot separate the colours for each one is integral to creating the other just like our inner coding and completion. Just by having an intention to revivify and re-member your beingness you shall begin a process that will organically be guided by the divine intelligence to reweave your spiritual spectrum back into balanced, enlightened wholeness. Do not try too hard: just follow your inner knowing, do the rituals and meditations as you feel guided to, trusting once again in the divine self that you are. Trust rebuilds that rainbow bridge back into the arms of love.

Archangel Metatron

AA Metatron and AA Sandalphon hold the polarities anchored for us. The Earth Gateway and Earth Star Chakra held by AA Sandalphon and the Cosmic Gateway and Soul Star Chakra held by AA Metatron. They are like twin brothers, the only two angels to have walked the earth as humans and ascended into the angelic realms. AA Zadkiel also works at the Soul Star on a more personal level.

AA Metatron vibrates through the Diamond Ray of intelligence; his force of Light is intense and powerful. This Diamond Light is a powerful force of energy to lift us into the arms of enlightenment. He is an angel of sacred presence, sitting on the right side of the Divine; he listens to the prayers and meditations of us all. He also holds the key to the Akashic records, working with our prayers and records to unwind and liberate our spirits. His pure ray of white reflects all others, even colours beyond our vision. As you become attuned to his ray you may find you start reflecting others unresolved issues. This can help them heal if they are willing to own it and not deflect it back to you. This is why it is so important to have a strong sense of yourself, to know who you are and who you are not. Develop good boundaries and ask for Metatron's help to balance this supernal light in your light body. He can help us rearrange our life to suit our new light code awakening, re-attuning the frequencies of light to create new experiences. Metatron has also been said to help with the New Age children arriving on the planet, to assist them to adapt their high frequency light bodies and also help with ADD type behaviour patterns and their overactive electrical systems. Call on AA Metatron to help your twelve helix DNA to heal and reactivate. He taught and supported these teachings back in the crystal temples of Atlantis, teaching the teachers and supporting the matrix of light to stay in tune with the higher councils and Divine Director. He was a channel of Divine wisdom, an anchor of pure intelligence and light, assisting in the creation of divine oracles to allow the divine communications to be continued.

Cosmic Gateway Crystals

Phenacite: probably one of the most powerful crystals around and is said to hold a very high frequency of light. Phenacite will access the light and silence of this gateway, especially if you program it to reach and work with this chakra. She will help bring this chakra's energy into alignment with your light body and physical body. Using it in meditation will help you access the information available to you through this chakra. It will instantly cleanse the light body and generate a pure white light that will activate all the higher, spiritual chakras. By opening the third eye with this stone you will be able to see and clearly move blockages to further expansion and growth. Accessing spirit guides is enhanced by this crystal.

Nirvana Quartz: so beautiful, instantly the energy of the Himalayan Mountains is felt as this is their source. The purity and profound peace it brings makes it one of my favourite crystals. It resonates in a place of no time, travelling beyond our perceived ideas of what life is about. She initiates a deep peace and quiet in the mind, shutting out the day-to-day trivia and expanding one's consciousness beyond into a space of sublime silence. I find working with this crystal takes me into lifetimes of prayer and solitude, connection to all things and yet at peace with it all. The name Nirvana resonates with enlightenment, which says it all. She can take us beyond the perceived ideas of life and open doors to new and wonderful possibilities.

Selenite: another all time favourite, selenite generates beautiful light, the striations along its length carrying the light through the nervous system and assisting with the transitions of healing and enlightenment we are going through. Owning a selenite wand is almost a must, such is its power to align our chakras with our light body and opening our higher chakras to allow more light to enter and activate them. Placing the wand along the spine will directly help the chakras, nervous system and vertebrae to align. Selenite looks otherworldly and as such opens these doors, taking us on spiritual journeys otherwise unavailable to us.

Diamond is the hardest of all the stones. The light is pure and reflects the diamond light body. Diamonds can activate the higher mind, burn through emotional issues and expand one's perception. There is sovereign energy to diamonds, giving the idea that they bring forth a graciousness of unconditional love and leadership.

Tanzanite helps us access messages from our guides and angels. It is a beautiful blue-violet colour, engaging our throat, third-eye, crown and higher etheric chakras, bringing them together so that we can more easily download the messages and knowledge available to us through these very high vibration gateways. The violet colour accesses the violet flame thus clearing any static or interference trying to undermine our clear connection to our higher guidance. She will enhance telepathy and other psychic gifts.

Flower Essence for the Cosmic Gateway

The Lotus

When I was given this essence I received guidance to call it Krishna's signature essence. It contains Phenacite, Selenite, Lemurian quartz, Kunzite and Amethyst as well as the lotus flower. All together they make a very high vibration mix, enabling an accessing of these higher chakras.

Master essence brings all the chakras, meridians and subtle bodies into temporary alignment.

Heals past DNA mutations caused by imbalances in how we have used our power.

Opens up the cells to release memories that are blocking your true self and spiritual gifts.

These gifts can then be downloaded into sub-conscious/conscious mind and one's light body.

Enhances the effects of other essences and herbal mixes, seems to amplify and activate the healing qualities.

Brings one's higher and lower nature into a harmonious balance, as above so below.

Fills you with spiritual light and earthly abundance, can be quite euphoric at times as you start to consciously feel these states of energy expanding within you.

Carries a gold/white ray energy

Good for lymphatic drainage, nervous system strengthening, endocrine system, heart, liver, spleen and blood tonic.

Works well with Krishna, AA Metatron and Sandalphon.

Use with other essences to enhance effects and lighten the energy when a bit of a boost is needed. Sometimes issues are not related to just one chakra. For example, with depression, lotus essence seems to exorcise the energy; the vibration clears the heaviness and lightens the load. Works like a "Doorway to Heaven". Lotus is a wonderful tonic for grief, cleansing and uplifting the loss and opening doors of consciousness to process the situation more comfortably. She may even allow for an easier communication with our loved ones who have passed over.

This is a wonderful essence to finish our journey with as Lotus seems to bring it altogether and amalgamate all our work. The lotus is one of my favourite symbols. She has roots deeply embedded in the mud and from this an absolutely radiant bloom arises, like our journey from 3D human to enlightened spiritual human, full and glowing with inner love.

Essential Oils to enhance Cosmic Gateway

The oils now are more about maintaining your light body and chakras so that a clear and ever-strengthening connection can be made and maintained. Essential oils are brilliant for this as they are so potent and pure, working on so many levels, from the physical through to the spiritual. They are derived from nature and carry a high vibration and potency. Buy a brand you feel is a good product. Sometimes I have overlapped the oils as they work with many levels of our being and fit with several of the chakras. Also there are no hard and fast rules. If an oil from an earlier chakra feels appropriate for working on a different area - go for it, because remember they are all intimately connected in their functioning.

Angelica is going to assist you to connect to your guides and angels. This oil creates a bridge of light, strengthening the connection between the physical and ethereal realms. It is balancing and protective which totally supports our spiritual connection. In using oils such as this we create a safe space for our pathways to the spiritual realm to grow stronger. It will filter the psychic pollution allowing for a clear and strong connection to evolve. Our goal is to create a conscious connection to the higher vibrational realms, to embody this state of being. This oil can help with that. Angelica also counteracts fatigue, stimulates the immune system and is a tonic for the nervous system, all important aids at this time.

Anise: this oil is also known as star anise. Anise clears the light body, the mind and emotions so that a clear connection with our higher self and guides can be made. When you feel your thoughts overcrowding your mental process, having a sniff of anise will bring a cleansing and clearing effect. Try burning some in an oil burner to clear your home and environment of stagnant energy and old thought forms. She will release constrictions in the etheric body caused by fear and anxiety thus attuning you back into the flow of your higher centres. It will align your chakras with the new frequencies to consciously ground the energy and manifest it in your physical life. Great for manifestation visualisations. Have a sniff and envision your dream, consciously bringing the vision into physical reality. As you work with this oil she expands your crown chakra allowing a clear and steady connection to be established. This will facilitate a more comfortable experience of awakening.

Cajuput: cajuput oil helps heal our inner child, our trust centre and innocence. She helps us feel safe again after all the trials of healing ourselves. Once this trust is re-established we can feel the devotional heart opening again to the light of our spirit and soul. Trust is a very important emotion to foster for it takes courage to take new leaps of faith on this very powerful and life-changing journey we are on. Sometimes nothing seems to be going as it should, things happen and strange opportunities arise to test us and take us on the next leg of our journey. It may not look anything like we think it should look but spirit is saying this is it, go this way. So have a sniff and blow those fears away and let that trusting child come out and play in the amazing new fields of life that are awaiting our willingness to engage with.

Peppermint: when all else fails. I just love peppermint, it cuts through everything leaving my mind, light body and chakras crystal clear and ready to see and deal with whatever is to be dealt with. By keeping one's light body clear you are so much more receptive to your higher guidance and connection to higher self. As we are still shifting through the last of our resistance and living in a world that still contains a fair amount of negativity, it is imperative to keep maintaining yourself. It is so important to do your cleansing and clearings so that your higher centres can keep growing stronger and guiding your pathway. Keep the flow of spiritual light going, work and maintain, be vigilant to your personal space and the higher ethereal chakras will sparkle and continue to work for you.

Complementary Oil Blends

A lovely blend for an all purpose uplifting, cleansing, purifying and spiritual oil would be:

Lemon: for increasing joy and optimism; sharpening one's awareness which enables spirit messages to be understood and materialised. Lemon will energise but calm one at the same time, lifting our vibration but calming so that we are receptive. Negative energies are repelled by lemon.

Frankincense: this will add a very spiritual upliftment to the blend, regeneration of health and access to spiritual insights and messages. Frankincense is quite protective also, clearing one's environment of negative influences as well as clearing one's personal space and light body.

Peppermint: as I have said this is a potent oil of upliftment, clarity and purification. The combination of the three creates a well rounded support for your spiritual work.

Another lovely blend for creating an atmosphere conductive for gentle healing and angelic contact:

Rose: rose will always attract the angels, guides and masters. It opens the heart, allowing it to receive guidance and healing, connecting you to your higher spiritual centres and enhancing meditation.

Neroli: neroli is an angelic oil, softening and opening the higher spiritual centres gently and lovingly. She will instigate self-actualisation which is at the heart of our spiritual journey.

Sandalwood: sandalwood will ground the mix, adding its own divine energy to the matrix. Sandalwood will strengthen the gifts of the other oils and add an ability to perceive subtle energy emanations, intuit messages from spirit, activate multi-sensory abilities and receive spiritual abundance.

Either blend a few drops of the essential oils with carrier oil like almond and use as anointing oil or place some drops of the blend in an oil diffuser and enjoy the atmospheric shift. Great for meditation space, healing rooms or to mix in with an incense blend.

Ritual of Activation for the Cosmic Gateway and Light Codes 49-64

A white candle

Sage or frankincense to cleanse space

Chosen oil for candle and anointing

Cosmic gateway sigil ... AA Metatron

Chosen crystal

Cosmic Gateway essence ... either taken orally, topically or by invoking the flower

Smudge your space or light some frankincense incense
Say prayer of protection

Place candle in a safe container with sigil either drawn on candle or placed underneath the candle holder

Anoint candle with oil

Have your crystal nearby, either hold it or place near candle

Take your essence, play some soft meditative music and relax. Do some deep, releasing breathing to bring yourself into a state of deep peace, feel open and receptive to the process of awakening.

Invoke AA Metatron

"In the name of love and light I ask my guides, celestial helpers and AA Metatron to please open, activate and balance my Cosmic gateway chakra, placing within it the crystalline structures and sacred geometries I need to fully bring my cosmic gateway chakra into its highest vibration and health activation. I ask that all the corresponding Light Codes 49 through to 64 be brought into harmony with my soul's highest expression now. I command the activation of the 49th through to the 64th light codes now, bringing them into their highest level of presence on every level of my light body and through every chakra and bodily system now. I ask that all my light codes come into harmony with each other, each supporting the harmonious action of the other as a unified whole. I am so grateful for this healing, thank you. Om Mani Padme Hum."

Be still, allow the process to be fuelled by its own momentum, knowing that your words are enough now to create change and invoke healing. Feel the white light flowing through out your light body, bringing in a new alignment and a whole new sense of self. Know your own guides and many angels are with you, surrounding you with their supernal light which is awakening your light codes to your own specific blueprint. Experience the deep flow of light throughout your body, weaving into your matrix to bring you into a whole new level of awareness. Soft gentle presence, loving caress of light, wings of love carrying you home into the arms of your own awaiting spirit.

Animal Totem

A flock of birds

Watch how a flock of birds in flight move as one, a unified field of intelligence, communicating silently as they swoop as one through the sky. This is how we will become, each one supporting the other, a telepathic knowing of the other's movements and thoughts, each supporting the other to create a positive and beauty full world. Communication silently projected across the earth, heard and experienced by the recipient, healing and messages received as a complete knowing, a nanosecond of time to send and receive, all happening right now. Be like the birds: a recognition of soul families and a unified consciousness only operating from a place of mutual love and support. All thoughts heard as clearly as words, so no thought, just movement in accord with the divine directive ... silence, knowing and grace.

Mantra

This mantra works with the goddess Bhuvaneshwari. This goddess is experienced as infinite space, stretching out forever, containing everything, luminous and boundless ... this is how the energy of Bhuvaneshwari feels. In meditation, she will be experienced as a motherly embrace and a formless state of awareness. Her mantra is wonderful to chant to open up that formless space to absorb fears and negative emotions. She is a goddess of sacred space, a mistress of all realities and a giver of grace. Call on her to experience a sense of full and sacred embodiment.

"Aum shrim hrim shrim bhuvaneshwarayai Namaha."

(Ohm shreem hreem shreem boo-van-esh-war-yai nuh-muh huh)

"Om, I offer salutations to the auspicious Lady of Space, manifestor of worlds."

This mantra works well with the final Light Codes, fully taking us into that formless space of the creator, activating our formless and luminous self.

Goddess Work

Sophia

Sophia is the goddess of wisdom; she is called by the ancients "Most Pure Mother of God". She was understood to be the womb of the Holy Spirit out of which was birthed the universe. As she birthed the layers of existence, she saturated them with the wisdom needed to survive and flourish. The Virgin Mary is said to be an embodiment of Sophia. Sophia will help us to discern true wisdom from false teachings masquerading as truth, thus assisting us to safely find our way back to our own personal pathway of ascension. There are and always have been many false prophets, feeding information to others in the hope of hooking people in to feed their false ego needs and unfortunately derailing others from their true pathway. Sophia teaches us to first listen to our own hearts: does what we hear make our heart sing or is there a wave of doubt or uncertainty? Always listen and discern what resonates with truth for you. Her symbol is the dove, a symbol of freedom through a pathway of the heart, of peace and gentleness. Learn to listen deeply to the song of your heart, learn how your heart communicates to you so that you can hear her warnings, her joy and wisdom. As you learn to recognise the inner messages, your own wisdom codes will re-ignite and will automatically alert you to what does not resonate with your energy and higher good.

Selfhood Meditation

"Sophia of the luminous light, cosmic mother and creator goddess

I pray to you to help me develop my inner wisdom
My inner codes of knowing, awakening to your truth and wisdom

That I may know truth from fiction, love from false murmurs

I ask that you activate my deepest heart knowing and self love capacity

And that this be my compass guiding me home to my truth

Filtering out that which does not serve my highest path of wisdom

That I now become an embodiment of this wisdom code

An expression of my own true selfhood and inner Sophia

Blessed Be, Om Mani Padme Hum."

This prayer can be spoken daily to invoke her holy presence and keep building a strong connection; it will strengthen your light body and the healing energy of awakening alive. Doing this will keep the divine filter of truth active, assisting your consciousness to learn how to recognise true experience from false. Sophia's energy is pure and alive so will really assist us to keep true to our own pure truth.

This process is called a daily devotional, something you do to set the tone of the day, to invoke a holy presence to accompany you.

When you get up in the morning or before bed at night, light a white candle, draw her sigil on the candle to strengthen the connection.

Have an essential oil or blend that you love and anoint yourself on the third-eye chakra.

Say the prayer with devotion and feeling, imagine her divine presence entering the space around you.

Breathe deeply of the scent of your oil, feel the light of the candle expanding its glow to surround you with heavenly light.

If you have any questions or concerns, allow them to be absorbed into the light of the candle where they are transformed by the love of Sophia.

Deeply feel into your sacred space, breathe the energy into your body, every cell expanding to embody your sacred self, feel the embodiment of this luminous aspect of yourself.

Rest as long as you feel the need in this sacred space. Know and trust that all uncertainties will be made clear as your day unfolds or as the night envelopes you in darkness and rest.

Wear your oil when experiencing doubt as a link to your inner Sophia. This will trigger and expose anything that you need to understand.

Say the prayer anytime, before meditation, sleep, to start the day or when you are in need of some support.

Always end the process by snuffing out the candle and knowing you are an expression of divine light. Leave the candle on your altar until your next devotional moment.

A Sacred Circle of Healing

This process was created to provide a sacred space for healing, either for yourself or another. As we evolve and progress into our enlightened bodies, the transmutation process can be uncomfortable. The body is throwing off old outdated programs and physical detoxing in the form of flu or other viruses can occur.

Also our environment is shifting; there is more negative energy often floating around as we all go through stuff. Deep illness can often be a karmic or genetic distortion that needs to heal. While all this is going on it is great to have a sacred and safe space where the energy is sealed, protecting us from further assault while we heal and regather our energy.

The invocation is about creating a circle around us but also a circle around every cell in your body, creating a protection as you go through the process of awakening your DNA and light codes. The four major archangels of the directions are called as are the lord and lady of the silver and gold rays (solar and lunar chakras). Into this sacred space you can work with your personal guides, crystal or plant devas and healing angels to create health and wellbeing. Use it as a pre-meditation invocation, then lie down and experience and visualise a perfect healing.

It can also be used with your medicine wheel to create a healing for another. Place their name in the centre of the wheel, then say the invocation, place any crystals on the circle points that you feel work for their health issues and herbs could also be added. Or place a tea light candle safely at the four directions, adding an appropriate essential oil to correspond with the direction and the intent.

For general healing and protection you could try:

East/air – lavender or bergamot; calming and uplifting

Crystal – clear quartz for intention and clarity

North/fire – Cedar wood, frankincense or rosemary; strengthening and protection

Carnelian – for energy and healing

West/water – Lemon, myrrh or thyme; cleansing and healing

Aquamarine – for emotional healing and balance

South/earth – Cyprus, geranium or vetiver; grounding and protection

Hematite – for healing, protection and grounding

These are just suggestions; there are many different options in this book. Select whatever your intuition feels is right for you at this moment.

Make a hole in the tea light candle with a sharp point and place a drop or two of the essential oil into the hole. As the candle melts the oil blends with the wax and releases the healing energy.

If you feel to, select one of the goddesses or masters that you wish to work with and place their sigil in the centre of the medicine wheel. Call in their assistance with one of the provided invoking prayers or make up your own to suit your intention.

If you are travelling, put your own name in the centre of the circle to keep you safe as you travel. The circle invocation can also used by those who are disturbed by astral spirits and wandering ghosts. Say the circle prayer then ask your guides and Archangel Michael to clear you and your personal environment of any lost souls, guiding them into the Light. Ask for your personal space to be sealed by the divine light of protection.

The Invocation

"I now invoke a heavenly circle

A healing temple of ethereal light

A boundary between good health and sickness

A circle filled with love, joy and peace

My own personal Shangri-la ... I Am

I call upon AA Raphael, guardian of clarity and healer in the east

I call upon AA Michael, guardian of protection and power in the north

I call upon AA Gabriel, guardian of the emotional waters in the west

I call upon AA Uriel, guardian of strength and manifestation in the south

Surround me now in my healing circle, assisting me to remove and clear all disease and darkness

In the name of the Silver Lady of Lunar Light and the Golden Lord of Solar Light

Do I now create and seal this healing circle

So be it."

See yourself surrounded by a luminous circle of Light, the archangels are blazing their light at the four directional points and your space is filled with positive, healing energy. Into this space invite your guides to assist you or just let go and allow what needs to be done to occur.

Simply by intending and invoking this circle you set in motion the energy that you need at this time for healing. As your higher chakras are now activated, you can relax into your personal space knowing that your higher self knows what is needed at this time for your highest good.

Invoke the circle as often as needed. Even if you say it before heading out into your daily life, it is a form of protection and preservation of personal space. Throughout the day see it in your minds eye, blazing its circle of light around you, allowing positive energy in but effectively sealing out what is of a more negative nature. It might look like an ultraviolet light that zaps anything that is not for your higher good. Understand this is also a circle of healing protection around you and within you, circling every cell in your body with cleansing and purifying energy. Say it before sleep at night as the energy will work with you as you sleep. If you suffer from bad dreams or find yourself waking up tired, a little astral protection may be needed. This circle prayer should help.

Summary of Light Codes 49 – 64

As we complete the awakening of these light codes we draw all the parts of ourselves back into a unified wholeness, one with our higher self, soul and the divine creator. Our matrix of light has unified with the cosmic self and we are now effectively operating as one, in accordance with the divine creator. We now know ourselves to be as one with all of life and yet still operating within our own beautiful individual self. Everything we need to know we just know, without trying. We just are as we are, now connected into the sacred web of light that connects us to universal knowingness. Our creativity is unique and divinely guided. Each one of us as integral to the creation process as the other, each role a part in the greater unfolding and creation of our beautiful world. It is now so important to watch your thoughts as now we are creative beings. Our higher light centres are now active and so they operate as receivers of cosmic data but also as transmitters of your thoughts … conscious and unconscious. So keep doing the exercises, saying the prayers and consciously being vigilant with yourself-care and maintenance. Be honest with self and what you are feeling. Honesty neutralises the energetic fallout of negative feelings; by being conscious and truthful you can navigate comfortably through these changes. No one expects you to be perfect. We are still human and we are still growing into a full integration of these changes, but by consciously working with yourself, watching your thoughts and maintaining your equilibrium you are effectively supporting the healing and upgrading of your neural pathways in the brain and creating a new and higher vibration to bring about a grounded and active shift.

Use your new upgraded system to create and manifest positively a better and more fulfilling life for yourself. Sit in the zero point of your higher self, feel the silence and envision financial abundance, great health and a beautiful and loving relationship. In this place of stillness and silence lies your pure potential. Within the stillness no ripples of doubt can interfere with your creation of pure potential. Explore and play with this new state of awareness. This is how we learn and grow, becoming an integration of these new beginnings. As our DNA heal and expand into their wholeness our world shall also heal as they are one and the same. Our DNA imbalances keep mother earth also in 3D limitation. Time to release the old and expand into the new, or more correctly, re-member the parts back into a divine whole.

A Final Blessing

The masters have given me a final mantra/prayer that comes from the fields of conscious oneness; this brings all the work into an integrated wholeness within us.

This is the language of the starry ones.

To Bring the All-Ness of the Journey into Oneness

This is a greeting and integration from the starry self:

 "Sham- bah – ha- lah - swaha

Shar mar ha lah

May ha, har lay

Shay ma tay ma hay."

She who shines like the stars

And bows before her own light

Offered as a mantra of peace

And whose gaze is filled with light now united forever more

As one with the flame of her divinity

It is now time to place the heart back into the seat of power ... Om Mani Padme Hum."

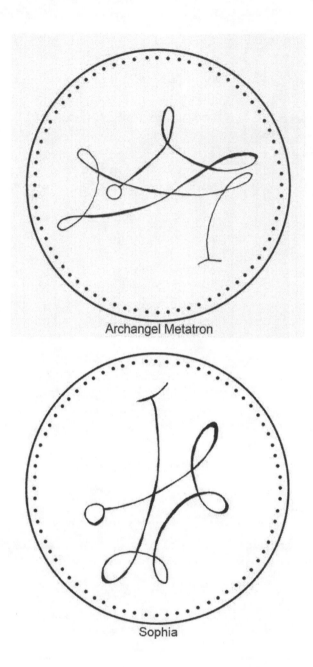

Appendix

How to Make a Flower Essence

I will keep this simple as there are many who have written on how to make a flower essence. There is a basic structure to the process; once you have that outline you can then dress up the making of it as you wish. For me, the making of it is a little ritual, creating a safe and protected space for the energetic infusion to occur as outside energies can influence the purity of the end result. Using the medicine wheel, provided in the book, as the mat to place the bowl on is a great idea as it provides angelic protection and empowerment. Crystals placed at the four directions adds an extra boost. Make sure you cleanse them and program them for the specific task you have in mind.

Making the Mother Essence

1. Tools needed: a clear glass bowl with no embellishments or a quartz crystal singing bowl is quite magical as you can sing it while the flowers are within it. A 100ml amber bottle to store the mother tincture in and a smaller 25ml or 15ml dropper bottle to store stock essence in.

2. A bottle of brandy to preserve the essence. This is used in the mother tincture, stock and dosage bottles.

3. Once you locate your flower remove it from the tree with a clean snip. Use nail scissors or slightly larger shears if needed. The main requirement is that it is quick and clean. I always ask the deva of the plant for permission to take the bloom and use it in my essence healing work. After the essence is made I pour some of it back into the earth with the spent blooms as a healing for Mother Earth and the plant deva.

4. Have spring water ready in your bowl and drop the bloom straight from your scissors into the bowl: it is best if you can avoid touching the bloom. Don't panic if you do touch it, I find it

usually all works out well.

5. Leave the bowl either near the plant in full morning sun or on your medicine wheel in a convenient place, as long as it is in full sunlight. The medicine wheel will preserve the integrity of the energy and the plant deva will also surround her flower and amplify her energy. Place 3-4 blooms in the bowl depending on their size. Some people only use the petals to avoid pollen and other bits floating into the mix but that is up to you. If you are using crystals, cleanse them and place them in the bowl prior to adding the flowers. I say a little prayer of thanks when I set the bowl as everything adds up to creating a sacred place to do your magical work.

6. Leave the bowl in the sun for a minimum of 3-4 hours depending on the intensity of the sun. You can test the energy with a pendulum if you wish; it is a good way to see when the essence has taken. The pendulum should do a nice clockwise swing to indicate a swelling of energy.

7. Fill the mother essence bottle with half brandy and half completed flower essence from your bowl. I use a turkey baster to remove the essence and safely place it in the mother bottle. Label the bottle with essence name and the date of creation - it is good to keep a record.

8. Take the stock bottle and fill it ¾ with brandy, 7 drops of mother essence and remainder with spring water.

9. To make up a remedy bottle for taking your essence over a longer period of time, fill 25ml bottle with ¼ brandy, 7 drops of stock essence and fill remainder of bottle with spring water. Take seven drops of this twice a day. Always succuss the bottle before taking as this re-energises the essence.

This Medicine Wheel is oriented for the Northern Hemisphere.

This Medicine Wheel is oriented for the Southern Hemisphere.

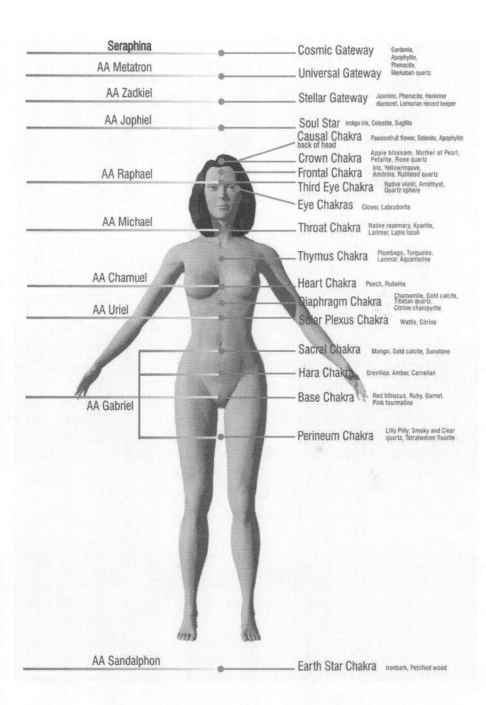

About the Author

Felicity Skye

My love of all things spiritual began around 25 years ago. Around that time I studied massage, counselling, meditation and flower remedies. I then went on to become a Reiki Master and shifted into doing spiritual healing and running meditation groups. Working in this way opened my spiritual sight and understanding; it has been such a privilege to have had the experiences and teachings I have received through my work.

Once my spiritual energy was established it was time to get my creative energy moving. I have created two oracle decks based on the teachings and visions I have received over the years. I did all the art for them as well as wrote the accompanying books. To this I have added a meditation CD and done personal spirit art for clients. My guides then directed me to make a series of flower/crystal essences which are included in my book. I also use them in my healing practice.

'Awakening Your Ancient DNA' is my first full length book. It started out as a six month workshop and ended up as a book and a set of sigil cards to go with it. This work is full of information I have gathered over the years and writing it was an amazing experience.

My spirituality has never been confined to just one pathway. I feel all paths have something precious to offer, so my work is always a weaving together of all my favourite bits from each path. Most of my work contains some Wicca, angelic prayer, sacred mantra, meditation and goddess ritual. Maybe this is symbolic of healing the separation that can even occur in spiritual practices and by weaving them into one we reweave our world and heal separation right at the spiritual core.

I am a mother of three, a wife; I have a dog that I adore and I live next to a beautiful beach on the north east coast of Australia. Nature surrounds me, it sings to my soul and makes every day a magical gift and healing.

Thank you for reading my book.

Felicity Skye

Connect with me:

Friend me on Facebook:

https://www.facebook.com/MagicalWorks

Bibliography

Anodea Judith, **Wheels of Life**, Llewellyn publications 2012

Deborah Eidson, **Vibrational Healing**, Frog Books, 2000

Kempton Sally, **Awakening Shakti**, Sounds True Books, 2013

Kryon, **The Twelve Layers of DNA**, Platinum Publishing House, 2010

Pearce Stewart, **The Angels of Atlantis**, Findhorn Press, 2011

Simmons Robert and Naisha Ashian, **The Book of Stones**, Heaven and Earth Publishing, 2005

Thomas Ashley-Farrand, **Shakti Mantras**, Ballantine Books, 2003

Made in the USA
San Bernardino, CA
24 February 2014